WRITING CLEARLY

AN EDITING GUIDE

Janet Lane and Ellen Lange

University of California, Davis

Heinle & Heinle Publishers
A Division of Wadsworth, Inc.
Boston, MA 02116 U.S.A.

The publication of *Writing Clearly: An Editing Guide* was directed by the members of the Heinle & Heinle ESL Publishing Team:

Erik Gundersen, Editorial Director
Susan Mraz, Marketing Manager
Kristin Thalheimer, Production Editor

Also participating in the publication of this program were:

Publisher: Stanley J. Galek
Editorial Production Manager: Elizabeth Holthaus
Associate Editor: Lynne Telson Barsky
Project Manager: Marjorie Glazer
Manufacturing Coordinator: Mary Beth Lynch
Photo Coordinator: Carl Spector
Interior Designer and Compositor: Barbara J. Goodchild
Cover Designer: Susan Schön

Heinle & Heinle Publishers is a division of Wadsworth, Inc.

Manufactured in the United States of America

Photograph Credits: Alicia Bruns/FPG, p. xxvi; Joseph Schuyler/Stock Boston, p. 26; Paul Conklin/Monkmeyer, p. 44; Harriet Gans/Image Works, p. 66; Rhoda Sidney/Stock Boston, p. 86; Michael Siluk/Image Works, p. 108; Lee Balterman/FPG, p. 126; David Wells/Image Works, p. 146; Michael Krasowitz/FPG, p. 162; Alan Carey/Image Works, p. 168; Spencer Grant/FPG, p. 180; Bob Daemmrich/Image Works, p. 196; Hazel Hankin/Stock Boston, p. 208; Joseph Schuyler/Stock Boston, p. 220; Howard Dratch/Image Works, p. 236

Library of Congress Cataloging-in-Publication Data

Lane, Janet.
  Writing clearly: an editing guide / by Janet Lane and Ellen Lange.
      p.   cm.
    ISBN 0-8384-3849-0
    1. English language--Textbooks for foreign speakers. 2. English language--Rhetoric. 3. Editing. I. Lange, Ellen. II. Title.
  PE1128.L3375 1993
  428.2'4--dc20   92-41830
                                                       CIP

ISBN 0-8384-3849-0
10 9 8 7 6 5 4 3 2 1

Contents

Preface to the Teacher

This book, *Writing Clearly: An Editing Guide,* is a course to help advanced ESL students become aware of common ESL language problems in writing and learn effective strategies for reducing these errors. The book guides students through 15 common ESL errors with a combination of explanations, selected grammar rules, self-help strategies, and exercises for practice, moving students from correcting errors in exercises to correcting them in their own writing. At the end of each unit, students have the opportunity to plan, write, and revise their own response to one or more writing topics and to edit what they have written for sentence-level errors. Students are also given the option to look for and correct errors in writing assignments in other courses they are taking.

Using this book, students will learn to analyze their specific sentence-level weaknesses and to develop strategies for improving their sentence-level control when they write. The ultimate goal of this book is for ESL writers to be able to rely on themselves when they write in English, rather than on the instructor or a native speaker.

This text has a companion book for the instructor entitled *Writing Clearly: Responding to ESL Compositions.* At the end of this preface, the contents of this instructor resource manual will be listed and the importance of using it will be explained. A complete answer key to the exercises in *Writing Clearly: An Editing Guide* is included in the companion book.

Options for Using *Writing Clearly: An Editing Guide*

Writing Clearly: An Editing Guide has great flexibility in that it can be used in several different teaching situations:

1. **As a course on its own** in improving language control in the context of writing.

   This textbook can be used as the sole text for a course in improving language control in writing. In this case, the instructor will most likely have the students do the writing assignments at the end of each unit.

2. **As a component of a writing course** where students are doing writing assignments outside of this textbook.

   This textbook can be used effectively along with a separate composition book and/or reader. In this case, the instructor may or may not choose to do the writing assignments at the end of each unit.

3. **As supplementary material** for ESL writers enrolled in a composition course geared toward native speakers of English, such as a college writing course for undergraduates or a technical writing course for engineers.

In this case, the instructor can use the symbols when marking an ESL student's paper. The instructor can have the student purchase *Writing Clearly: An Editing Guide* and meet with the instructor to set priorities for working on errors. The student can then work individually using the explanations and exercises in the units suggested by the instructor.

Options for Ordering the 15 Units in *Writing Clearly*

The 15 units in this book have been designed for use in either consecutive or nonconsecutive order.

1. **Instructors who plan to use the entire book**
   a. Instructors may choose to go straight through the units in the order they appear, beginning with the first nine units, which cover more serious (global) errors, and proceeding to the final six units, which cover less serious (local) errors.
   b. Alternatively, they may choose the units according to the needs of the class. In this case, the instructor should still focus on global errors first, since these are the errors that affect meaning most. However, this does not mean that an instructor should not teach a local error, such as subject-verb agreement, early in the course if the students particularly need it.

2. **Instructors who plan to use the book selectively** can make their choice of units to be taught based on the needs of the class. Again, it is recommended that global errors be covered first.

3. **Instructors who have students working individually with the book** can have a student either work straight through the book or do selected units based on the student's needs.

How to Cover the Units in the Text

The Time Required for Covering the 15 Units

The 15 units in this book can be covered in 15 weeks assuming five hours per week of class time. Alternatively, the book can be covered in less time if some material is either omitted or assigned for students to do at home. An effective way to reduce the class time spent on each unit is to focus on doing the exercises in *Part III* during class and to spend less class time on *Part II*.

Each unit of the book can be covered in approximately four to six class hours. Generally speaking, units that cover one major grammatical point, such as conditional or subject-verb agreement, can be covered more quickly than units that cover several grammatical points grouped into one major category, such as sentence structure or verb form. Two units, unclear and nonidiomatic, are much shorter than the other 13 units and can be covered in less time.

What follows is a suggested plan for working through a unit in the text.

Suggested Plan for Working Through a Unit

Hour 1

Before class

Students read *Part I* and then answer the "Test Your Understanding" questions.

During class

Go over the students' answers, respond to any questions students may have, and emphasize points in *Part I* that you feel are especially important. Begin *Part II* by summarizing each problem, for example, or by having students read the correct sentences aloud in each problem.

Hour 2

Before class

Students read *Part II*.
Students choose their writing topic (*Part IV, Step 1*).

During class

Continue with *Part II*. Go over guidelines and rules in *Part II* to make sure students understand them.
Students gather information on their writing topic in small groups (*Part IV, Step 2*).

Hour 3

Before class

Students do prewriting (*Part IV, Step 3*).
Students do selected exercises in *Part III*.

During class

Finish *Part II*, making sure students identify which problems they commonly have with the error explained in the unit.
Continue with exercises in *Part III*.

Hour 4

Before class

Students write their first draft (*Part IV, Step 4*).
Students complete exercises in *Part III*.

During class

Finish going over exercises in *Part III*.

Students share their drafts (*Part IV*, Step 5).

Hour 5

Before class

Students revise and proofread their draft (*Part IV*, Steps 6–7).

During class

Students turn in final draft.

Finish anything outstanding from the unit and preview new unit.

Note: Part V can be done at the teacher's discretion, depending on whether or not the students are doing writing assignments outside of the topics in the book.

Other Important Information for the Instructor

The List of ESL Grading Symbols

The list of ESL grading symbols covers 15 common ESL errors divided into two parts: global errors and local errors. Each error corresponds to one of the 15 units in *Writing Clearly: An Editing Guide*. Also included on the list are symbols for ten errors commonly made by native speakers; some ESL writers also will have problems with these errors. This group of errors is not covered in this book.

The Global/Local Error Distinction

Some errors are much more serious than others and can seriously affect the reader's ability to understand the content of a piece of writing. You will want to have your students work on these serious errors first. The list of ESL Grading Symbols in this book is divided into two parts to distinguish more serious errors from less serious ones. You will note that the nine errors listed in the top box of the list are usually the most serious errors. They are called **global** errors because they usually affect more than just a small part of a sentence as well as the reader's understanding of the writer's ideas. In contrast, the six errors in the middle box of the list are less serious errors. They are called **local** errors because they usually affect a smaller part of a sentence and, while they are distracting, generally do not affect the reader's understanding.[1]

It is very important to keep in mind that, in some cases, the global/local distinction may not always be clear. That is, an error that is usually local, such as nondiomatic writing, could become global if it affects a large portion of a text. Some types of global errors, such as leaving off the *-ed* ending of a past

---

1. The terms *global* and *local* come from M. K. Burt and C. Kiparsky's *The Gooficon: A Repair Manual for English*. Rowley, Mass., Newbury House, 1972.

participle, might be considered less serious than other verb-form errors by some instructors. Although this global/local error distinction is designed to help you make decisions about how serious an error is, you will sometimes need, or want, to make your own decisions concerning how serious a certain error is in a given piece of writing.

Options for Using the Grading Symbols

1. In responding to students' writing, the instructor may choose to mark on students' papers several types of errors starting at the beginning of the course, keeping in mind the guidelines given in *Chapter 3* of *Writing Clearly: Responding to ESL Compositions* for choosing the most serious errors to mark and giving high priority to errors that occur frequently. The instructor thus uses the units to focus in on specific problems according to the needs of the students in the class.
2. Some instructors may choose to mark only the error covered in a particular unit when responding to students' writing or to mark the errors covered in previous units as well as the error of the unit being covered.

The Error Awareness Sheet

In addition to the grading symbols, you may want to use the Error Awareness Sheet on page xxii to help your students become aware of what their errors are and to help them decide which errors to work on first.[2] You can mark this sheet yourself or have the students record their errors after you have returned a paper to them. The Error Awareness Sheet has complete instructions at the top on how to use it.

The Scope of This Book

The focus of *Writing Clearly: An Editing Guide* is error analysis rather than comprehensive grammar study. Although each unit includes selected grammar rules and self-help strategies for working on reducing errors, students are often encouraged to consult additional references such as an advanced ESL grammar text or an ESL dictionary to increase their knowledge of a particular grammatical point.   Students are also encouraged to increase their knowledge of English by reading as much as possible. Specific instructions on how to make effective use of their reading are given to students throughout the units. The pedagogical reason for encouraging students to work independently is to make students rely more on themselves and less on their instructor, tutor, a peer, or a native speaker for help with sentence-level accuracy in their writing.

---

2. The term *Error Awareness Sheet* was used by J. F. Lalande in "Reducing Composition Errors: An Experiment." *Modern Language Journal*, 66, 140–149.

How to Use the Writing Topics

In *Part IV* of each unit, the number of writing topics varies from two to six. The instructions invite students to choose one or more topics for writing. Instructors may want to assign one or more topics depending on factors such as time constraints and whether or not *Writing Clearly: An Editing Guide* is being used as the main text for the course or as a supplementary text to a writing course that has given writing topics of its own.

In the instructions for the writing topics in *Part IV*, no length is suggested for the writing topics so that the instructor may elect to have students write a paragraph or several paragraphs in response to a topic. Instructors can make this decision depending on the level of the class, the amount of time allotted to each unit, and the function of the text (main text or a supplementary text) in the course.

The writing topics have been chosen to elicit the error covered in the unit as much as possible. However, instructors will want to encourage students to respond to the topics naturally rather than to focus on incorporating the grammar point taught in the unit. Such an approach to the topics will help students see that the primary focus in writing is on content and will prepare them for future writing tasks in the academic and professional worlds—tasks that are not focused on a particular grammar point.

The Value of Getting a Diagnostic Writing Sample

At the first or second meeting of the class, it is highly recommended that the instructor have the students do a writing sample similar to the type of writing they will be doing in the class. The instructor can use this diagnostic in several ways:

1. **To determine the needs of the class overall and those of individual students.**

   The diagnostic will show what the students' strengths are as well as their weaknesses, including what sentence-level errors they make.

2. **To give the students an overview of the grading symbols.**

   After returning the marked diagnostic, the instructor can briefly explain the meaning of the different symbols and indicate that each will be explained more fully during the course.

3. **To help the teacher decide on an order for teaching the units based on class needs.**

The Benefits of Using the Teacher Sourcebook with *Writing Clearly: An Editing Guide*

Writing Clearly: Responding to ESL Compositions (the teacher sourcebook) differs from a standard teacher's manual that suggests how to use a student text because it offers instructors an overall system for responding to their ESL students' writing in terms of both content and sentences. It includes the following information that is essential for responding effectively to ESL writing:

- how to respond to content in an ESL paper
- how to respond to sentences in an ESL paper
- how to assign grades to an ESL paper
- how to help ESL students benefit from the instructor's feedback on content and sentences

For responding to sentences, it provides instructors with an effective and efficient system, including a set of 15 grading symbols that can be used to respond to sentence errors accurately, clearly, consistently, and selectively. These grading symbols correlate with the 15 units in the student book.

While instructors could use the student book alone, simply adopting the 15 grading symbols listed and explained in it to mark papers, this approach to sentence-level marking would not necessarily be the most beneficial method for helping ESL students improve their writing. Instead, instructors will find it more beneficial for the student if they respond to sentences within the greater context of responding to content, as well as within the context of encouraging student analysis of errors, both of which are explained in practical and theoretical terms **only** in the teacher sourcebook. In addition, instructors who simply adopt the method of using the 15 grading symbols in the student book will not benefit from the explanations in the teacher sourcebook of how to use these grading symbols.

Thus, the system offered in the teacher sourcebook for responding to ESL students' writing is an effective method to help ESL students improve their language control and to encourage them to develop strategies for reducing sentence-level errors in their writing.

Preface to the Student

In the academic and professional worlds, writing is very important. For all writers in these situations, native and nonnative speakers alike, content and language control are important. For ESL writers, however, achieving sentence-level accuracy is doubly challenging because English is not their native language.

As an ESL writer, you are, of course, subject to making language errors when you write. While making errors is a natural part of learning a second language, you will need to work on eliminating these errors, particularly in formal writing. There are good reasons why you must worry about sentence-level accuracy. When you are doing academic writing, or any kind of formal writing, you must take into account that the readers' demands and expectations are very high. Readers of formal written English are aware not only of content but also of sentence-level accuracy, and they expect sentences to be correct. Also, when your writing contains ESL errors, you run the risk of either not getting your meaning across to the reader or causing the reader to be distracted from the content of what you have written because of the language errors. Therefore, as an ESL writer, you cannot rely solely on content and ignore the need for sentence-level accuracy in your work.

Although getting back a paper covered with marks indicating there are problems can be discouraging, you must keep in mind that your instructor's feedback can be extremely valuable. When you read your instructor's comments on your drafts or final drafts, you can become aware of strengths in your writing as well as problems to focus on while writing your next paper. Receiving feedback on your writing will be easier if you view your instructor positively, keeping in mind that he or she is not merely a judge or a hunter of errors but an interested reader of your work who wants to help you learn to write effectively.

Acknowledgments

We are indebted to our students at the University of California, Davis, whose interest in achieving language control in their writing prompted us to write this textbook. We are also grateful to the Undergraduate Instructional Improvement Program of the Teaching Resources Center at the University of California, Davis, for partially funding the writing of the *Resource Manual for Responding to ESL Compositions* for the Composition Program in which an earlier, much smaller version of this material was included.

During the process of writing this textbook, we have been fortunate to have had the encouragement and guidance of the staff of Heinle and Heinle, including Erik Gundersen, editor, and Lynne Telson Barsky, associate editor, whose unfailing support helped us transform our manuscript into a textbook. We are also indebted to Kristin Thalheimer, production editor, for skillfully overseeing the project. Our deepest appreciation goes to our project manager, Marjorie Glazer, whose excellent suggestions strengthened the text and whose enthusiasm for exactness motivated us as writers.

We also wish to thank Peter Master, of California State University, Fresno, who provided valuable feedback on the unit on articles and Linda Bates, our colleague at the University of California, Davis, who commented on many of the units. We are also indebted to those students who so generously contributed their sentences, paragaphs, and essays as examples for this textbook.

Most importantly, we had the unwavering support of significant people in our lives: Harry, Peter, and Carolyn—for Ellen; Bashira, Susan, Emil, and Jason—for Janet. Without their constant support, this book would not have been possible.

Introduction

Part I: How to Use Your Instructor's Feedback Effectively

Understanding Your Instructor's Symbols

In order to improve your sentence-level accuracy, you will first need to know what kinds of errors you are making. One way to find out what your errors are is to look at the symbols your instructor has written on your paper. These symbols, which indicate what your errors are, are often abbreviations (such as ss for sentence structure). In *Part III* in this introduction, you will find a list of ESL grading symbols and an explanation of each symbol. By examining the symbols on your paper and checking them against this list, you will be able to find out what your errors are. If your instructor is not using the symbols in this book, or if he or she is using additional symbols, you will need to find out exactly what your instructor's symbols mean.

Deciding Which Errors to Work on First

Once you know what your errors are, you must prioritize them and not try to work on all of them at once. Some errors are much more serious than others because they can interfere with the reader's ability to understand the content of your writing. You will want to work on these errors first. The ESL Grading Symbols in *Part III* of this introduction will help you learn which errors are more serious and which are less serious. The nine errors listed in the top box are the most serious errors. They are called **global** errors because they usually affect more than just a small part of a sentence, and they usually affect the reader's understanding of your ideas. The six errors in the middle box of the list are usually less serious errors. They are called **local** errors because they usually affect a smaller part of a sentence and while they are distracting, they generally do not affect the reader's understanding.[1] The ten errors in the bottom box are commonly made by native speakers. If you are having problems with these errors, you will also need to work on them.

Keep in mind that, in some cases, the global/local error distinction may not be clear. That is, an error that is usually local, such as nonidiomatic, could become global if it affects a large portion of a text. Some types of global errors (such as leaving off the *-ed* ending of a past participle) might be considered less serious than other errors within the same category (in this case, verb form).

---

1. The terms *global* and *local* come from M. K. Burt and C. Kiparsky's *The Gooficon: A Repair Manual for English*. Rowley, Mass., Newbury House, 1972.

In order to make the most progress in improving your sentence-level accuracy, you will want to prioritize your errors according to their seriousness. If you find that your instructor has marked most of your errors **vt** (verb tense), **vf** (verb form), **art** (article), and **num** (number), you will want to work on the two global errors, verb tense and verb form, first. You will also need to consider the frequency of your errors. If you are making many global errors, it would be best for you to start working on those global errors that you are making most often; likewise, if there is a certain local error that you are making quite frequently, it would be wise for you to work on this error also, especially if you are not making many global errors.

Your instructor may assist you in deciding which errors to work on first by helping you prioritize your errors. For example, your instructor might write at the end of your paper that you need to work on sentence structure and verb-tense errors first. Or your instructor might fill out a checklist for you such as the Error Awareness Sheet in *Part III* of this introduction.[2] If your instructor fills out this Error Awareness Sheet, he or she will tally your errors for you in the middle column so that you can see how frequent they are. In the right column your instructor will indicate which of these errors you should begin working on first. Alternatively, your instructor may have you fill out the Error Awareness Sheet yourself.

Part II: Strategies for Working on Your Errors

Using the 15 Units in This Book

Once you know what your errors are, you can use the 15 units in this book to find out more about each error and how to correct it. Each unit treats one sentence-level error ESL writers commonly make. In each unit, you will find a short introduction to the error, which defines the error, explains why it is important to avoid the error, and suggests ways to master it. Following the introduction, you will find problems that ESL writers commonly have with that error. In this section you are given incorrect sentences to show you the error along with the appropriate correction. In addition, selected grammar rules and self-help strategies are given to help you learn how to master the error. These rules and strategies, however, are not meant to be comprehensive, so you may sometimes want to increase your knowledge of a particular grammatical point by studying it in depth in an ESL grammar text or by looking up a word in an ESL dictionary. In each unit, you will also find exercises to help you test your ability to identify and correct the error and produce grammatically correct sentences of your own. You will also find a writing activity in each unit, which your instructor may or may not assign. This writing

---

2. The term *Error Awareness Sheet* was used by J. F. Lalande in "Reducing Composition Errors: An Experiment." *Modern Language Journal*, 66, 140–149.

assignment is designed to help you move from correcting the errors in someone else's writing to mastering the errors in your own writing.

In using the units, you should always read all of *Parts I* and *II* in order to discover exactly what your individual problems are. For example, if you are making sentence-structure errors, ask yourself whether your problem is omitting the verb *to be* as in *I happy* or doubling the subject as in *My friends and I we like ice cream*. If you can use the units in this way to discover just what aspects of the error you need to work on, you will increase your chances of avoiding the error in your writing. The selected grammar rules and self-help strategies in each unit will also help give you the background you need to avoid making errors.

Setting Realistic Goals

As you work on your errors, remember to set realistic goals for yourself. Do not try to work on all your errors at once. Even if you can eliminate only two or three of your most serious and frequent errors, your writing should improve significantly.

Revising Your Writing by Yourself or with a Tutor

Once you have decided which errors to work on and have read about them in this textbook, a good strategy for improving your sentence control is to revise each sentence containing these errors. When you revise each sentence, do not write out the incorrect sentence; instead, write out only the new, correct sentence. By writing out the entire sentence and not just part of it, you will be more likely to remember the correct pattern. If you are working with a tutor, you can share your corrected sentence with the tutor. You can also ask the tutor to check your essays in progress for errors of the type you frequently make. You can then work with the tutor on finding and correcting those errors. In working with a tutor, you can also do extra exercises on the errors you are making, using exercises from an ESL grammar text or those provided by the tutor.

Becoming an Independent Self-Editor

Once you are aware of and know how to correct your most serious and frequent sentence-level problems, you must monitor for them when you write. Monitoring means consciously trying to avoid making these errors when you are writing, or going back and correcting them once you have made them. In other words, you are becoming alert to the errors you know you are likely to make when you write in English.

You should decide whether you find it easier to monitor while you are writing or to go back and check for certain errors after you have completed a piece of writing. Of course, the end goal is for you to write without making these errors. But remember that reaching this goal will take time. Thus, until you are able to avoid making these errors, you need to be consciously aware of them and monitor for them during your writing process. Again, remember to set realistic goals for yourself. It will probably not be possible for you to monitor for all of your errors at once, especially if you are writing under time pressure. You might, for example, choose to monitor only for sentence-structure and verb-tense errors in a piece of writing if you know these are your most serious errors.

By learning to monitor in this way, you will become an editor of your own writing, and you will find that you have to rely far less on your instructor, a tutor, or a native speaker for help with your writing.

Part III: Grading Symbols, Error Awareness Sheet, and Sample Paper

ESL Grading Symbols

GLOBAL ERRORS—more serious errors
(These errors usually impede understanding.)

SYMBOL	EXPLANATION	PAGE*
vt	incorrect verb tense	1
vf	verb incorrectly formed	27
modal	incorrect use or formation of a modal	45
cond	incorrect use or formation of a conditional sentence	67
ss	incorrect sentence structure	87
wo	incorrect or awkward word order	109
conn	incorrect or missing connector	127
pass	incorrect formation or use of passive voice	147
unclear	unclear message	163

LOCAL ERRORS—less serious errors

(These errors, while distracting, most often do not impede understanding.)

SYMBOL	EXPLANATION	PAGE*
sv	incorrect subject-verb agreement	169
art	incorrect or missing article	181
num	problem with the singular or plural of a noun	197
wc	wrong word choice, including prepositions	209
wf	wrong word form	221
nonidiom	nonidiomatic (not expressed this way in English)	237

*Note: The pages listed in the right-hand column refer to pages in **Writing Clearly: An Editing Guide,** where a full explanation of each error is given.

OTHER ERRORS

(These errors are commonly made by native speakers.)

SYMBOL	EXPLANATION
cap	capitalization—capital letter needed
coh	coherence—one idea does not lead to the next
cs	comma splice—two independent clauses joined by a comma
dm	dangling modifier—phrase or clause with no word(s) to modify in a sentence
frag	fragment—incomplete sentence
lc	lower case—word(s) incorrectly capitalized
p	punctuation—punctuation incorrect or missing
pro ref pro agree	pronoun reference/agreement—pronoun reference unclear or agreement incorrect
ro	run-on—two independent clauses joined with no punctuation
sp	spelling error—word incorrectly spelled

Error Awareness Sheet

Directions: This Error Awareness Sheet will help you to discover what your sentence-level errors are and to learn to prioritize them. Put a check in the second column for each error marked on your returned paper. Then, from the most frequent errors in the second column, select two or three that you can begin working on first and put a check next to them in the third column. Always remember that you need to work on frequent global errors first.

Name of Student: Essay:

TYPE OF ERROR	TOTAL NUMBER OF ERRORS	TOP-PRIORITY ERRORS TO WORK ON
GLOBAL ERRORS (more serious)		
vt		
vf		
modal		
cond		
ss		
wo		
conn		
pass		
unclear		
LOCAL ERRORS (less serious)		
sv		
art		
num		
wc		
wf		
nonidiom		
OTHER ERRORS		
cap		
coh		
cs		
dm		
frag		
lc		
p		
pro ref/agree		
ro		
sp		

Sample Paper

Writing topic: Discuss the progress you have made so far on your English 25 term-paper assignment. In addition to explaining what you have already done and what you are currently working on, comment on the aspect of writing a term paper that has been most challenging for you.

    After five weeks of studies at this university, I learned many skills from *(vt)* ᴀEnglish 25 course. One of the most important is writingᴀterm paper. I *(art)(art)* would like to write something about my term paper right now.

    I scheduled my term-paper writing progress into ten parts: 1) deciding *(vt)(wc)* topics, 2) collecting reference papers/books, 3) briefly reading those *(num)* papers/books, 4) writing *down* the outline, 5) reading the papers/books *(vf (v + no prep))* carefully and taking notes, 6) writeᴀfirst draft, 7) revising the draft, 8) *(vf)(art)* asking my tutor to comment on my paper, 9) typing it, and 10) finally checking the paper. So far, I finished the first four steps and is proceeding to *(vt)(sv)* the fifth step. I hope I can speed up; otherwise it will be very busy on the *(pro ref)(wc)* end of November because [it dues] on December 4. *(ss)*

    In order to type my term paper, I must learn how to operate Macintosh or PS/2 computers because I never use them before, especially two kinds of *(vt)* packages (Word 5.0 for Macintosh and WordPerfect for PS/2). As a result, I attended several lab classes offered byᴀcomputer center. It is really interest- *(vt?)(art)(pro ref)* ing and I enjoyed it very much. It is useful for my future career too, and I *(pro ref)(pro ref)* think it is most challenging to me in writing my term paper. *(pro ref)*

In this response, you have done a careful job of addressing both parts of the question and have illustrated your points with good specifics, including the names of word-processing programs. Good organization, too!

Because your organization is strong, I have marked most of your sentence-level errors as you requested. I would suggest, however, that you first work on verb tense and articles. Also, you will want to work on avoiding unclear refer-ences when you use the pronoun it.

Error Awareness Sheet: Filled Out for Sample Paper

Directions: This Error Awareness Sheet will help you to discover what your sentence-level errors are and to learn to prioritize them. Put a check in the second column for each error marked on your returned paper. Then, from the most frequent errors in the second column, select two or three that you can begin working on first and put a check next to them in the third column. Always remember that you need to work on frequent global errors first.

Name of Student: **Essay:**

TYPE OF ERROR	TOTAL NUMBER OF ERRORS	TOP-PRIORITY ERRORS TO WORK ON
GLOBAL ERRORS (more serious)		
vt	✔✔✔✔	✔
vf	✔✔	
modal		
cond		
ss	✔	
wo		
conn		
pass		
unclear		
LOCAL ERRORS (less serious)		
sv	✔	
art	✔✔✔	✔
num	✔	
wc	✔✔	
wf		
nonidiom		
OTHER ERRORS		
cap		
coh		
cs		
dm		
frag		
lc		
p		
pro ref/agree	✔✔✔✔	✔
ro		
sp		

To our students
whose desire to write clearly
was the inspiration for this book

UNIT 1: VERB TENSE*

*vt = grading symbol for verb-tense errors

■ PART I: What You Need to Know About Errors in Verb Tense

> **In Part I, you will answer the following questions:**
> - What is an error in verb tense?
> - Why is it important to avoid verb-tense errors in writing?
> - What are some strategies for mastering verb tenses?

Definition of the Error

Verb tense refers to the time the verb expresses. The form of the verb *ride* in the sentence *We rode our bicycles to campus* indicates that the time of the action of riding our bicycles was in the past, not in the present or the future. A verb-tense error (**vt**) may result from the incorrect choice of a verb tense within a sentence or from the inappropriate shifting of verb tenses within a paragraph or group of paragraphs.

Errors marked verb tense (**vt**) may also relate to **aspect**. Aspect refers to some characteristic of an event or action beyond its time. For example, both of the following sentences describe actions that take place in the present. The difference is one of aspect: *Matt studies in the library in the evening* and *Matt is studying in the library this evening*. The verb in the first sentence shows a habitual action, whereas the verb in the second sentence shows a temporary action that is happening right now.

There are also different aspects in past time as illustrated by the following sentences: *I was working on my essay yesterday* and *I worked on my essay yesterday*. While both sentences describe actions that are in past time, only the first sentence emphasizes the duration of the action. The present perfect tense also shows aspect. In the sentence *Alicia has moved to a new apartment*, the act of moving has already occurred, but the use of the present perfect indicates that the action occurred close to the present time. In the sentence *Alicia moved to a new apartment*, the use of the past tense indicates that the moving occurred at a definite time in the past.

Importance of Mastering Verb Tenses in Writing

Verb-tense errors are global (more serious) errors. Because time is an important message expressed by the verb in English, a writer must be able to control verb tenses in order for the reader to understand when actions and events take place. In addition, as explained earlier, some verb tenses communicate other information such as duration (as opposed to the completion of an event in the past). (*The phone was ringing* rather than *The phone rang*.)

If you do not control verb tenses, your readers will have difficulty following the sequence of events in your writing.

Suggestions for Mastering Verb Tenses

To make sure you understand the uses of verb tenses in English, review the verb-tense chart in *Part II* of this unit. In particular, review the present perfect tense carefully. Not only is this verb tense frequently used in English, but it is also often one of the most difficult tenses for ESL students to master.

Remember that in English, even when you have a time word or phrase (such as *last week*, *tomorrow*, or *yesterday*) stated in a clause or sentence, the verb must also express time as in the sentence *We went to the movies yesterday*.

Moreover, throughout a piece of writing, you will need to be aware of the sequencing of verbs. Watch for unnecessary shifts in tense, yet also be aware that you will often need to use several different verb tenses. The sample paragraphs in *Parts II* and *III* of this unit will guide you in using different verb tenses in a passage.

Another useful strategy for becoming aware of the variety of verb tenses that can occur in a piece of writing is to examine the verb tenses in your academic and leisure reading material. As you examine this written material, note that when a writer shifts to a different verb tense, this shift is often signaled by a time-reference word or phrase, such as *when I was in high school*, *yesterday*, or *tomorrow*. These words prepare the reader for a shift from one time frame to another.

TEST YOUR UNDERSTANDING OF VERB TENSE

After you have read *Part I*, write answers to the questions below. Share your answers with another student.

1. What is an error in verb tense? Explain in your own words.
2. What is aspect, and why is it important for ESL writers to know about it?
3. How serious are verb-tense errors?
4. Do you tend to make verb-tense errors when you write in English? If so, which verb tenses are a problem for you?
5. In your native language, are verb tenses used to show time in the same way they are used to show time in English?
6. What strategies can ESL writers use to avoid verb-tense errors in their writing?

■ PART II: Common Problems, Rules, and Self-help Strategies

> ### In Part II, you will
> - *study two problems ESL writers commonly have with verb tenses*
> - *study the forms and uses of verb tenses in English*
> - *learn strategies for controlling verb tenses within a piece of writing*

This section presents two problems that ESL writers commonly have with verb tenses. First, study each problem and the examples that illustrate it. Then mark the problems you think you have when you write in English. Remember that if you become aware of the types of verb-tense errors you make most often, you will increase your chances of avoiding these errors in your writing. *Note:* As you study these problems, you may find it helpful to refer to the verb-tense charts on pages 10–18.

PROBLEM 1. An incorrect verb tense has been used in a sentence or clause.

Incorrect:	Alex <u>has sent out</u> several job applications last month.
Correct:	Alex <u>sent out</u> several job applications last month.
Explanation:	The action of sending out the applications has been completed. Thus, the simple past tense is needed.
Incorrect:	I <u>was</u> in the United States since 1985.
Correct:	I <u>have been</u> in the United States since 1985.
Explanation:	The action of being in the United States started in the past and has continued into the present. Thus, the present perfect tense is needed.
Incorrect:	At the moment I live in the dormitory, but I <u>decided</u> to move into an apartment next year.
Correct:	At the moment I live in the dormitory, but I <u>have decided</u> to move into an apartment next year.
Explanation:	Since the decision to move into an apartment has been recently made, the present perfect tense is needed.
Incorrect:	Students <u>pay</u> less tuition last year than this year.
Correct:	Students <u>paid</u> less tuition last year than this year.

Explanation:	Less tuition was paid by students last year. Thus, a past-tense verb is needed to agree with the time expression, *last year*.
Incorrect:	Yosemite Park <u>was</u> one of the most popular of all of the national parks.
Correct:	Yosemite Park <u>is</u> one of the most popular of all the national parks.
Explanation:	The comment about Yosemite Park is a general statement that is true in the present. Thus, the present tense is needed.
Incorrect:	Many students <u>participate</u> in the commencement ceremony next month.
Correct:	Many students <u>will participate</u> in the commencement ceremony next month.
Explanation:	The commencement will take place next month. Thus, a future tense verb is needed to agree with the time expression, *next month*.

Self-help Strategy: To avoid verb-tense errors, make sure the verb tense you use fits the time you want to express. For example, if you are writing about something that will happen in the future, your verb should express future time. Also, remember that even when the time is indicated with a time word, such as *yesterday*, *today*, or *tomorrow*, the verb must still show the time of the action.

When the time is not explicitly stated, you will need to think carefully about the time you are trying to express. In the following sentence, the time is not stated in words, yet the writer is remembering a past action **now**. Thus, the verb *remember* is in the present tense even though the verbs *had* and *went* are in the past tense.

	[right now] [past] [past]
Example:	I remember the fun we had when we all went to Disneyland.

PROBLEM 2. The verb tenses within a piece of writing (one or more paragraphs) inappropriately shift from one time frame to another.

Incorrect:	Although this is my first year in college, I have already found that there <u>were</u> some differences between high school and college. One of the things I <u>learned</u> in college is that a person has to be independent.
Explanation:	Since the writer is in his or her first year of college, he or she appropriately started out in the present time frame (*is*, *have found*). However, the writer then inappropriately shifts to the past (*were*, *learned*) instead of staying in the present.

Correct: Although this is my first year in college, I have already found that there <u>are</u> some differences between high school and college. One of the things I <u>have learned</u> in college is that a person has to be independent.

Note: As the verb sequencing in the following example shows, sometimes it is appropriate to shift from the present to the past. This is especially common when the writer is giving an example from the past.

Incorrect: Most students have many expectations and ideas about college before they actually enter. Some of these expectations are similar to reality, yet some are quite different. Before I started college, I <u>have imagined</u> [*vt*] how the classes and teachers would be and came to the conclusion that they <u>will</u> [*vt*] not be any different from high school.

Explanation: The writer appropriately begins in the present with two general statements. However, the writer needs to shift to the past when writing about an experience that took place before she started college.

Correct: Most students have many different expectations and ideas about college before they actually enter. Some of these expectations are similar to reality, yet some are quite different. Before I started college, I <u>imagined</u> how the classes and teachers would be and came to the conclusion that they <u>would</u> not be any different from high school.

TEST YOUR UNDERSTANDING
OF VERB-TENSE SEQUENCING

First, find the shift from the present to the past tense in paragraphs A & B. Then determine whether or not the shift in each paragraph is appropriate.

A.   Many men in my country still do not encourage their wives to work outside the home because they think women are not able to do anything but housework. However, these men were wrong. They will never know what their wives can do or who their wives can be.

B.   Personal computers have become very important tools in both homes and offices. At home people use them for everything from writing letters to keeping records of their monthly budget or for doing their income taxes. In the workplace, computers are used for word processing, for sending messages, for computer-aided design, for writing software, for locating reference material, and for doing numerous other tasks. Before homes and offices had personal computers, individuals had to type and retype drafts of letters and other material. Engineers and others had to draft and design using pen, paper, and drawing boards. Students, researchers, and librarians had to search for reference materials manually. Producing and locating all this material took much longer in those days than it does now. From writing to designing to communicating, computers have made our lives easier in both the home and the workplace.

Now compare your answers to the following:

Answer to A: The shift to the past is **not** appropriate because the writer is still commenting in general about men in his country. The writer thinks that these men are generally wrong in their opinion. **General statements that are true in the present require the simple present tense.**

Answer to B: The shift to the past tense is appropriate because the writer shifts from a discussion of what is true in the present to a discussion of what it was like **before** personal computers became common. Shifting into the past tense is necessary to make the comparison between present and past.

Strategies for Mastering Verb-Tense Sequencing

You will usually need to use several different verb tenses in a piece of writing. Examine the verbs in the following two passages carefully and note how various verb tenses can work together in sequence.

Passage 1: Present Focus

In the following passage, the principal time focus is the present; however, the writer can also look back to the past and forward to the future, using the present as a frame of reference.

> I am glad to be living in Davis, a small college town in northern California between Sacramento and San Francisco. Known as the bicycle capital of California, Davis has many facilities for bike riders, including bike lanes on almost every street, bike racks in front of almost every store and office, and special traffic-light buttons for cyclists. I enjoy being able to ride my bicycle to school everyday. Also, because Davis is a university town, I can choose to attend many interesting events, such as lectures, movies, and cultural performances. I am never bored! Although I moved here only six months ago, I already feel at home and have made many good friends. I know I am going to enjoy the rest of my stay in Davis, even though I do not know how long I will remain here.

Notes on Time Focus in Passage 1

NOW—Present

I <u>am</u> glad to be living in Davis.

Davis <u>has</u> many facilities for bike riders.

I <u>enjoy</u> riding my bicycle to school.

Davis <u>is</u> a university town.

I <u>can choose</u> to attend many interesting events.

I <u>am</u> never bored!

I <u>feel</u> at home here.

PAST—Before the present

I <u>moved</u> here only six months ago.

PAST AND PRESENT—Started before the present and is still happening now

I <u>have made</u> many good friends.

FUTURE-—After the present

> I <u>am going to enjoy</u> the rest of my stay.
>
> I do not know how long I <u>will remain</u> here.

Passage 2: Past Focus

The following passage is centered around a past event. Notice, however, that the writer shifts tenses several times—to describe events further in the past (before this event), in the present, and in the future.

My cousin Ron decided to drop out of college two weeks ago. Apparently, he had been depressed for about two weeks prior to making this decision. I understand he had been having financial problems that had led to marital problems as well. Ron's classmates encouraged him to speak with his professors or a counselor, but unfortunately Ron refused. His classmates and his family feel terrible that they could not convince him to get counseling before making the decision to quit school. They are worried that eventually Ron will regret his decision and will wish he had stayed in school.

Notes on Time Focus in Passage 2

PAST

> My cousin <u>dropped out</u> of college two weeks ago.
>
> His classmates <u>encouraged</u> him to speak to his professors or a counselor.
>
> His classmates wish they <u>could have convinced</u> Ron to seek counseling.

EARLIER THAN THE PAST

> Ron <u>had been</u> depressed.
>
> He <u>had been having</u> financial problems. (*Note:* The past perfect progressive emphasizes the **duration** of these problems.)
>
> His financial problems <u>had led</u> to marital problems.

PRESENT—Now, after the event

> I <u>understand</u> Ron had been having financial and marital problems.
>
> His classmates <u>feel</u> terrible and <u>wish</u> they could have convinced him to seek counseling. (*Note:* present wish about a past event)
>
> They <u>are</u> worried he will regret his decision.

FUTURE—After the present time

> Ron's family and classmates are worried that Ron <u>will regret</u> his decision and <u>will wish</u> he had stayed in school.

Forms and Uses of Verb Tenses in English

The following charts provide an explanation of the forms and uses of verb tenses in English. You may want to begin by reviewing all of the tenses. Then study more carefully those tenses that you find difficult.

SIMPLE PRESENT

When can you use this verb tense?

Use	Examples
To express a habitual or repeated action in the present or a condition that is true at any time.	Thuy rides her bicycle to school everyday. I am not a morning person. In fact, I usually do not get up until 10:00 A.M.
To express general truths that are timeless (well-known laws or principles or even generally accepted truths about people, places, and customs).	Water boils at 100 degrees Celsius. Generally speaking, Spaniards eat dinner much later than Americans do. University students often do not get enough sleep.
To report what appears in print. This use is common in academic writing when the writer is referring to texts and quotations. In the example, even though Norman Cousins wrote his article in the past, the writer has put the underlined verb in the present tense.	In his article, "The Communication Collapse," Norman Cousins asserts that schools encourage poor writing habits by forcing students to write under time pressure. (*Note:* The writer could also use the past tense, *asserted*.)
To describe past events as if they were happening now. This use is called the **historical present**. In the example, taken from a longer account of a visit to Nepal, the writer has chosen to narrate his adventures using the present tense, even though the trip is over and he is back in the United States.	My friend and I arrive at Kathmandu Airport on February 25, 1991. Jim meets us with a taxi, and we drive to what is to be our apartment for nearly three weeks. The drive is culture shock number one.

SIMPLE PRESENT, *cont.*

How do you form this verb tense?

> ➤ base form of the verb (infinitive without *to*) or, for third-person singular, add *-s* or *-es*

Examples: I write
you write
we write
he/she/the student writes
they/the students write

PRESENT PROGRESSIVE

When can you use this verb tense?

Use	Examples
To express an action or activity that is happening right now (at this moment, today, this year); the action has begun and is still happening.	Tammy <u>is working</u> on the first draft of her essay. Monica <u>is majoring</u> in aeronautical engineering.
To express that an action or activity is happening at the present time and is temporary.	Mark <u>is working</u> for his uncle. (Allows for the possibility that Mark may not permanently work for his uncle.)
To express an action that is already in progress at a specified point of time in the present.	When my roommate gets home after class, I <u>am</u> usually <u>cooking</u>. At 8:00 P.M., Teresa <u>is</u> usually <u>studying</u> in the library.

How do you form this verb tense?

> ➤ am/is/are + present participle *(-ing)*

Examples: I am reading
you are reading
he/she/the student is reading
we are reading
they/the students are reading

SIMPLE PAST

When can you use this verb tense?

Use	Examples
To indicate that an action or event took place at a specific time in the past.	I <u>visited</u> Japan in 1991. Last night we <u>saw</u> a movie about India.
To indicate that an action or event occurred over a period of time in the past with the implication that it is no longer true in the present.	I <u>lived</u> in Los Angeles for 15 years. Barbara <u>was</u> on the volleyball team in college.

How do you form this verb tense?

➤ Regular verbs: base form + -*ed*

Examples: I walked
you walked
he/she/the student walked
we walked
they/the students walked

Note: Many verbs have irregular past-tense forms. Some common irregular past-tense forms include *took, ate,* and *came.* Consult an ESL grammar book for lists of common verbs that have irregular past-tense forms. You can also find irregular past-tense forms in the dictionary under the base form of the verb.

PAST PROGRESSIVE

When can you use this verb tense?

Use	Examples
To express that an activity was in progress at a specific point of time in the past.	At 8:00 last night, I <u>was studying</u> in the library. I <u>was cooking</u> when the phone rang.
To show that an activity lasted for a period of time in the past (emphasis on the duration).	I <u>was working</u> all day yesterday. I <u>was cooking</u> while you <u>were sleeping</u>.

How do you form this verb tense?

➤ was/were + present participle (-*ing*)

PAST PROGRESSIVE, *cont.*

Examples: I was reading
you were reading
he/she/the student was reading
we were reading
they/the students were reading

PRESENT PERFECT

When can you use this verb tense?

Use	Examples
To express an action or state that began in the past and continues in the present.	Hiroaki <u>has lived</u> in California for two years. I <u>have known</u> Hiroaki since he came to California.
To indicate that an action or event occurred some time in the past, although the exact time is not specified or important.	Veronique <u>has moved</u> back to France. I <u>have</u> already <u>filed</u> my income taxes.
Note: This tense can also indicate that an event has very recently happened. The adverb <u>just</u> is often used in this case.	I <u>have</u> just <u>completed</u> the math problem set.
To indicate that an action or event has occurred more than once in the past (specific times are not given or important).	Susan <u>has seen</u> the doctor several times about her allergy problem.

How do you form this verb tense?

➤ has/have + past participle

Examples: I have walked
you have walked
he/she/the student has walked
we have walked
they/the students have walked

Note: Many past-participle forms are irregular (for example, *known, seen, written, met*). Check an ESL grammar book for lists of common verbs that have irregular past-participle forms. You can also look up irregular past participles of individual verbs in the dictionary, under the base form of the verb.

PRESENT PERFECT PROGRESSIVE

When can you use this verb tense?

Use	Examples
To emphasize the duration of an activity that started in the past and has continued into the present.	I <u>have been waiting</u> for you for an hour. Abdulaziz <u>has been living</u> in California for two years.
To indicate that an activity has been in progress recently (the activity started in the past and is still going on).	Ramon <u>has been reading</u> the book *War and Peace*. I <u>have been thinking</u> about moving out of the dorm.

How do you form this verb tense?

> ➤ has/have + been + present participle (*-ing*)

Examples: I have been waiting
you have been waiting
he/she/the student has been waiting
we have been waiting
they/the students have been waiting

PAST PERFECT

When can you use this verb tense?

Use	Examples
To indicate an action that was completed by a definite time or before another action was completed in the past.	In English class I suddenly realized that I <u>had forgotten</u> to bring my textbook. I <u>had</u> never <u>read</u> anything by Jane Austen until last month.
Note: If the word *before* or *after* is in the sentence, the simple past may be used instead of the past perfect.	After all my friends <u>left</u> (or <u>had left</u>), I cleaned up the apartment.

PAST PERFECT, *cont.*

How do you form this verb tense?

> ➤ had + past participle

    Examples: I had called
you had called
he/she/the student had called
we had called
they/the students had called

Note: Many past-participle forms are irregular (for example, *written*, *met*, *known*). Check an ESL grammar book for lists of common verbs that have irregular past-participle forms. You can also look up irregular past participles of individual verbs in the dictionary under the base form of the verb.

PAST PERFECT PROGRESSIVE

When can you use this verb tense?

Use	Example
To emphasize the duration of an activity that was completed before another action or time in the past.	I <u>had been waiting</u> for him for an hour when he finally arrived.

How do you form this verb tense?

> ➤ had + been + present participle (*-ing*)

    Examples: I had been waiting
you had been waiting
he/she/the student had been waiting
we had been waiting
they/the students had been waiting

FUTURE

When can you use this verb tense?

Use	**Examples**
To express an action, event, or state that will occur in the future.	I <u>will drive</u> you to the airport tomorrow. Terry <u>will graduate</u> next June.

How do you form this verb tense?

> will + base form

Examples: I will attend
you will attend
he/she/the student will attend
we will attend
they/the students will attend

Note: Do not use an -s on the base form of the verb in the third-person singular.

Other Important Information about Expressing Future Time

Future time can also be expressed in the following ways:

> am/is/are going to + base form

Examples: We <u>are going to take</u> the midterm on Friday.
The city <u>is going to have</u> a parade on July 4.

> simple present or present progressive (especially with verbs of arriving and departing)

Examples: The plane <u>leaves</u> at 8 P.M. this evening.
The plane <u>is leaving</u> at 8 P.M. this evening.

When the future is expressed in a sentence that is in past time, *will* becomes *would*.

Examples:

1. **present/future time:** The instructor <u>says</u> that the exam <u>will cover</u> the first five units of the textbook.

   past time: The instructor <u>said</u> that the exam <u>would cover</u> the first five units of the textbook.

2. **present/future time:** Even though I plan to go to college next year, I <u>do not know</u> how demanding college classes <u>will be</u>.

   past time: When I <u>was</u> still in high school, I <u>did not know</u> how demanding college classes <u>would be</u>.

FUTURE PROGRESSIVE

When can you use this verb tense?

Use	Examples
To express an action that will be happening over a period of time at some specific point in the future.	Even though <u>I will be studying</u> when you call, I do not mind being interrupted.
To emphasize the duration of an action in the future.	Lin <u>will be working</u> on this essay for the next week.

How do you form this verb tense?

➤ will + be + present participle (*-ing*)

Examples: I will be leaving
you will be leaving
he/she/the student will be leaving
we will be leaving
they/the students will be leaving

FUTURE PERFECT

When can you use this verb tense?

Use	Examples
To indicate that an activity will be completed before another event or time in the future.	Maria <u>will have finished</u> her Ph.D. by the time she leaves for a two-year stay in France. We <u>will have finished</u> five essays by the end of the semester.

How do you form this verb tense?

➤ will + have + past participle

Examples: I will have gone
you will have gone
he/she/the student will have gone
we will have gone
they/the students will have gone

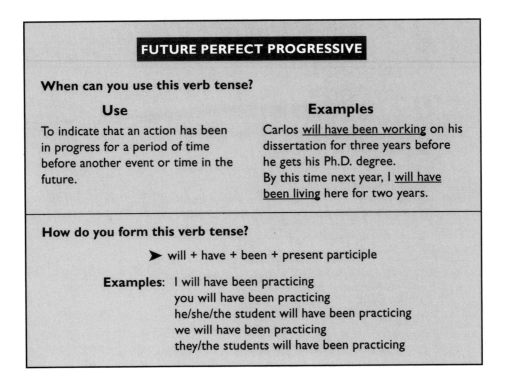

FUTURE PERFECT PROGRESSIVE

When can you use this verb tense?

Use	Examples
To indicate that an action has been in progress for a period of time before another event or time in the future.	Carlos will have been working on his dissertation for three years before he gets his Ph.D. degree. By this time next year, I will have been living here for two years.

How do you form this verb tense?

➤ will + have + been + present participle

Examples: I will have been practicing
you will have been practicing
he/she/the student will have been practicing
we will have been practicing
they/the students will have been practicing

■ PART III: Exercises

In Part III, you will practice

- *recognizing and correcting verb-tense errors in sentences*
- *using verb tenses correctly in a paragraph*
- *recognizing and correcting verb-tense errors in several paragraphs*

EXERCISE 1 (Do this exercise on your own. Then check your answers with a classmate.)

Directions: Examine each verb tense in the following sentences to decide whether or not a sentence is correct (C) or incorrect (I). Cross out each incorrect verb and write the correct verb above it. Be prepared to explain why your choice of verb tense is correct.

Example: __I__ Since I have been a college student, I ~~made~~ *have made* many new friends.

_____1. I was interested in physics since high school.

_____2. Having computer skills is essential for a college freshman, and I decide to learn how to use a computer.

_____3. Roger majors in environmental engineering on this campus.

_____4. Since she was a child, she likes sports, especially water sports, such as swimming and water skiing.

_____5. The civil engineering department has just received a large grant to do research on wastewater management.

_____6. Mario graduate as a veterinarian in January 1989.

_____7. Hector speaks Spanish and comes from Costa Rica.

_____8. Human beings make mistakes. Sometimes we did things we greatly regretted.

_____9. It was raining all day yesterday.

_____10. The professor had given an introduction to the course yesterday, the first day of class.

_____11. There are rumors that tuition is higher next year.

_____12. For the rest of the term, we will be learning about writing term papers.

_____13. By the time of the presidential election, the candidates will have campaigned in most, if not all, of the fifty states.

_____14. My Ph.D. research takes a great deal longer than I expected.

_____15. In my opinion, voting in elections was very important.

EXERCISE 2 (Do this exercise on your own. Then check your answers with a classmate.)

Directions: First read the entire paragraph. Then fill in each blank with the correct verb tense of the verb in parentheses. *Note*: For some verbs, more than one option is possible.

One quality that (help) _____*helps*_____ students succeed in their

studies is self-discipline. Self-discipline (be) _____ particularly important in college. I (learn) _____ a great deal about self-discipline by observing two of my friends. I have noted that my roommate Betsy (plan) _____ her time every night before she (go) _____ to bed. She (write) _____ down what she (have) _____ to do the next day and how much time she (spend) _____ doing each activity. First, she (schedule) _____ time for attending classes and working. She also (set) _____ aside time for socializing, running, studying, and eating. By having a timetable and sticking to it, Betsy (is) _____ always able to accomplish a lot more than I can. Another friend, Jo, (discipline) _____ herself by not doing anything unless she (complete) _____ all of her homework and reading. One night last semester, I (invite) _____ her to go out to dinner, but she (refuse) _____ because she (not finish) _____ her physics problem set. I wish I could be as disciplined as these two friends of mine are. I (know) _____ that self-discipline is important if I want to be successful in college. Thus, next term I (make) _____ an effort to discipline myself.

EXERCISE 3 (Do this exercise with a classmate.)

Directions: The following paragraph, written by a student, has been edited so that the only errors are in verb tense. First, read the paragraph. Then cross out each incorrect verb and write the correct verb tense above it. *Note*: For some verbs, more than one option is possible.

I have a positive attitude toward writing in English. When I first came

to America, I was very confused about using English, a new and strange

went OR has gone
language. But as time ~~goes~~ by, my feeling toward the language begin to

change. I force myself to write even though it was hard at first. I write a

lot, and I become more confident each time I write. Now, although I am more confident about writing, I still have many problems to overcome. I find that writing takes a great deal of time and one has to be patient and disciplined in order to be good at it. At times, I was frustrated and impatient with my writing. In fact, sometimes I sit for hours and cannot write even a word. Nevertheless, despite my frustration and long hours of work, I tend to have a positive attitude toward writing in English. Even though English is not my native language, I have found that I simply like to write.

EXERCISE 4 (Do this exercise on your own. Then check your answers with a classmate.)

Directions: The following paragraph, written by a student, has been edited so that the only errors are verb-tense errors. First, read the paragraph. Then cross out the incorrect verbs and write the correct verb tense above each incorrect verb. *Note:* In some cases, more than one option is possible.

function
Children of immigrants who do not speak English often ~~functioned~~ more like adults than children. As a child of immigrant parents myself, I have often had to act as an adult. Ever since my family arrived here five years ago, I take care of them in many ways. I have had to pay the rent, the utilities, the telephone, and any other payments. I translated letters from English to Italian for the whole family. When a family member was sick, I had gone along to the doctor to explain the problem and to translate the doctor's suggestions. I believe it has been good for me to do all these things because it prepared me for what I face when I am living on my own. Having adult responsibilities gave me the chance to understand what the world is like outside of my home. It provided me with hands-on training and is beneficial for me.

EXERCISE 5 (Do this exercise on your own. Then check your answers with a classmate.)

Directions: The following paragraph, written by a student, has been edited so that the only errors are in verb tense. First, read the paragraph. Then cross out each incorrect verb and write the correct verb tense above it.

Luckily for me, at the very end of my first semester here at college, my grades changed for the better. My Chemistry 1A class last semester is one example. At the start of the semester, I did not understand the materials or the problems. I was confused when I read and ~~try~~ *tried* to solve problems. Even though I do the homework and go to all the laboratory sessions, my understanding did not seem to improve. In fact, on my first and second midterms, I receive a D and an F. After receiving those two grades, I start to realize that I had to change the way I was studying. I decide to put myself on a strict schedule and to go to the library every day after dinner. I continue to follow this plan until the end of the semester. Even now, I still cannot believe how well I had done on my final. I received a B on the final and a C for the semester. This is what I think happen: When I reviewed all the materials systematically, I am able to understand principles of chemistry that I did not understand before.

EXERCISE 6 (Do this exercise on your own.)

Directions: Choose an article in a newspaper or magazine. After reading the article, underline all the verbs in one or two paragraphs. Do you understand why the different verb tenses were used? If you are unsure of any of them, ask a classmate, a tutor, or your instructor.

■ PART IV: Writing Activity

> ## *In Part IV, you will*
> - *plan and write a response to one or more topics*
> - *share your writing with a classmate*
> - *edit your writing for content and sentence-level accuracy*

Step 1—Choosing a Writing Topic

Select one or more of the following topics:

Topic A: Write about your career plans and goals. First, describe the education and/or training that you have already received and that which you still hope to obtain. Then explain how you hope to use this education and/or training in the future.

Topic B: Write about an interesting place you have visited. This place may be one which you have visited only once or twice (such as a tourist attraction) or a place where you regularly go (such as a café, restaurant, or bookstore). First, describe this place and explain what people do there. Then explain why you would recommend that others visit this place.

Topic C: Write about a historical event that had or has had major effects, either positive or negative, on your country. First, explain the event. Then analyze its effects, making it clear whether you see these effects as positive or negative.

Topic D: Write about what you did during your last vacation from school or work. In addition to explaining what you did, evaluate this vacation in terms of how enjoyable and/or profitable it was for you. To what extent was the vacation what you had hoped it would be?

Topic E: Write about what you see yourself doing next year. Where do you think you will be and what do you think you will be doing?

Topic F: In his book, *The Seven Habits of Highly Effective People*, the author S. R. Covey (Simon and Schuster, 1990) writes about what makes people successful. Whether or not you have read this book, you probably have your own ideas about what makes a person highly effective or successful. Write one or more paragraphs to explain your ideas on this subject. What habits or characteristics do you think are important for a person's success? (***Note:*** You may wish to narrow this topic to what makes a person in your field of study or research successful.)

Step 2—Gathering Information

Once you have selected a topic, discuss it with a classmate or in a small group. If you have chosen Topic B, for example, discuss the place that interests you. Discuss what people do there and why you think others would enjoy going there.

Step 3—Prewriting

Working by yourself, list some of the ideas you have discussed with a classmate or in a group.

Step 4—Writing Your First Draft

Use your list from prewriting to help you write your first draft. Focus on content.

Step 5—Sharing Your Draft

Working with a classmate, read each other's draft. Give feedback to each other using this format:

A. Reading for Content

1. What did you like most about this paper?
2. What would you like to know more about?
3. What suggestions do you have for the writer?

B. Checking for Problems in Verb Tense

1. Circle or underline any verb-tense problems you notice in your classmate's draft.
2. Discuss how to correct them.

Step 6—Revising Your Writing

Using your classmate's suggestions as well as your own ideas for revising, write your second draft. Focus on content and sentence-level accuracy. As you check each sentence, be especially aware of the verb tenses you have used. You may want to underline each verb in one or more paragraphs of your draft. Then check whether these verbs are correct in tense and form.

Step 7—Proofreading Your Final Draft

Read your final draft once again, paying particular attention to verb tenses. Make any necessary changes.

Postwriting Activity

Step 1—When your paper is returned, check to see if your instructor has marked any verb-tense errors.

Step 2—If so, review the material in *Part II* of this unit.

Step 3—Correct each verb-tense error by rewriting the sentence in which the error occurs. If you are unsure of a correction, ask your instructor or a classmate for help.

■ PART V: Applying What You Have Learned to Other Writing Assignments

> **In Part V, you will**
>
> • *look for and correct verb-tense errors in other writing assignments you have already completed*

If you are in a composition class or another class in which you do written assignments, take your last returned paper and follow these directions:

1. Check whether your instructor has marked any verb-tense errors on your paper. If so, try to correct them, using the material you have learned in this unit as a guide.

2. If your instructor has not marked any verb-tense errors, take one paragraph and underline each verb. Try to determine whether each verb is correct in tense and form. If you are not sure, ask a classmate or your instructor to help you.

3. When you do writing assignments in the future, be sure to check for accuracy in verb tense.

UNIT 2: VERB FORM*

*vf = grading symbol for verb-form errors

■ PART I: What You Need to Know About Errors in Verb Form

In Part I, you will answer the following questions:
- *What is an error in verb form?*
- *Why is it important to avoid verb-form errors in writing?*
- *What are some strategies for mastering verb forms?*

Definition of the Error

A verb-form error (**vf**) is an error in the formation of a verb. For example, the verb form is incorrect in the following sentence: *We have not yet <u>estimate</u> the cost of the trip*. Here, the past participle *estimated* is needed instead of the base form *estimate*. The form of the verb *enroll* is incorrect in the sentence *Mona has decided <u>enrolling</u> in three courses this semester*. The verb following *decide* must be the infinitive *to enroll*.

Note that verb-form errors with modals, the conditional, and the passive voice are not covered in this unit but rather in the units on modals, the conditional, and the passive. Also, present and past participles used as adjectives are covered in *Unit 14* (Word Form). However, errors involving prepositions associated with certain verbs (*I am <u>interested in</u> contemporary art; I just <u>hung up</u> the phone*) are addressed in this unit.

Knowing the following terminology will help you understand the material on verb forms contained in this unit.

an infinitive
   to walk, to study, to speak

a base form
   walk, study, speak (the infinitive without *to*)

a gerund or present participle
   walking, studying, speaking

a past participle
   walked, studied, spoken

a simple past form
   walked, studied, spoke

a verb phrase
   has been speaking, has spoken, am speaking, will have spoken (a main verb along with any auxiliary verbs)

Importance of Mastering Verb Forms in Writing

Verb-form errors are global (more serious) errors and will usually affect the meaning of a text considerably. Furthermore, problems with verb formation are greatly distracting to the reader because verbs are such an important part of a sentence in English. Because readers in the academic and professional worlds expect verb formation to be correct, incorrect verb forms make a piece of writing, no matter how strong the content is, appear flawed to the reader.

Suggestions for Mastering Verb Forms

Some verb-form errors, such as those involving incorrect formation of part of a verb phrase, can be avoided by studying grammar rules. For example, the underlined verb in the sentence, *He has send out several resumés*, is incorrect. The writer of this sentence needs to learn that the formation of the present perfect is [have/has + past participle] not [have/has + base form]. If you are making such errors, you will want to study the rules for verb-phrase formation given in this unit.

Other verb-form errors (those involving prepositions that follow certain verbs and verbals following verbs) are not governed by rules but are similar to a vocabulary problem. If you are making these kinds of errors, you will need to memorize individual cases just as if you were learning a new word. For example, you might have to learn that certain verbs, such as *dislike*, are always followed by a gerund (the *-ing* form) as in *I dislike running*, while other verbs, such as *hope*, are followed by an infinitive as in *I hope to run*. Still others, such as *like*, can be followed by either a gerund or an infinitive as in *I like running* or *I like to run*. The list of verbs in this unit will help you recognize and master these verb forms.

Keep in mind that you cannot depend upon your ear to help you master verb formation because in spoken English it is often difficult to hear exactly how a verb is formed. For example, it is difficult to hear the difference between *talk* and *talked* in spoken English. Thus, listening to the spoken language will probably not help you learn that the correct verb phrase is *she has talked* rather than *she has talk*. Likewise, because auxiliary verbs are most often unstressed (not said loudly or clearly) in spoken English, your ear will probably not help you distinguish between the correct *I am going* and the incorrect *I going*.

It is, however, extremely useful to become aware of verb formation when you read. Newspapers, magazines, textbooks, and other written material can be excellent resources for examples of correct verb formation.

Part I, continued

TEST YOUR UNDERSTANDING OF VERB-FORM ERRORS

After you have read *Part I*, write answers to the following questions. Share your answers with another student.

1. What is an error in verb form? Explain in your own words.
2. How serious are verb-form errors? Explain your answer.
3. Do you think you make verb-form errors when you write in English?
4. What strategies can ESL writers use to avoid making verb-form errors?

■ PART II: Common Problems, Rules, and Self-help Strategies

In Part II, you will

● *study six problems ESL writers commonly have with verb formation*
● *learn selected rules and self-help strategies that will help you control verb forms in your writing*

This section presents six problems ESL writers commonly have with verb formation. First, study each problem and the examples that illustrate it. Then mark the problems you think you have when you write in English. Remember that if you become aware of the type of verb-form errors you most often make, you will increase your chances of avoiding these errors in your writing.

PROBLEM 1. The main verb has been incorrectly formed.

Incorrect: My comment <u>hurted</u> my roommate's feelings.

Correct: My comment <u>hurt</u> my roommate's feelings.

Incorrect: She <u>flied</u> to Los Angeles for Chinese New Year.

Correct: She <u>flew</u> to Los Angeles for Chinese New Year.

Self-help Strategy: If you wish to study lists of the most common irregular verb forms in English, you will find them in most ESL grammar books. If, however, you are unsure of the forms of only a particular verb, you can look the verb up in a dictionary. Most dictionaries list irregular verb forms under the base form of the verb.

PROBLEM 2. Part of the verb phrase has been incorrectly formed.

Note: A verb phrase is a main verb with one or more auxiliary verbs.

Incorrect: Susan <u>did not received</u> the letter I wrote her.

Correct: Susan <u>did not receive</u> the letter I wrote her.

Incorrect: Ben did not want the teacher to know that he <u>had not study</u> for the quiz.

Correct: Ben did not want the teacher to know that he <u>had not studied</u> for the quiz.

Rules for Verb-Phrase Formation

By learning the following rules for verb-phrase formation, you will increase your chances of avoiding verb-form errors when you write.

DO (do, does, did) + BASE FORM

Examples: She <u>does</u> not <u>know</u>.
She <u>did</u> not <u>know</u>.
I <u>do</u> not <u>know</u>.

HAVE (have, has, had) + PAST PARTICIPLE

Examples: She <u>has left</u>.
She <u>had</u> already <u>left</u> when I arrived.
I <u>have</u> already <u>left</u>.

**BE (am, is, are, was, were, have been, has been, had been)
+ PRESENT PARTICIPLE**

Examples: She <u>is sleeping</u>.
She <u>was sleeping</u>.
She <u>has been sleeping</u>.
She <u>had been sleeping</u> for an hour when I arrived.
I <u>am sleeping</u>.
We <u>were sleeping</u>.
We <u>have been sleeping</u> for an hour.

PROBLEM 3.   The form of a verbal following a verb is incorrect.

Incorrect: He decided g̲o̲i̲n̲g̲ to the library tonight.

Incorrect: He decided g̲o̲ to the library tonight.

Correct: He decided t̲o̲ ̲g̲o̲ to the library tonight.

Incorrect: Matthew avoided t̲o̲ ̲d̲i̲s̲c̲u̲s̲s̲ that issue.

Incorrect: Matthew avoided d̲i̲s̲c̲u̲s̲s̲ that issue.

Correct: Matthew avoided d̲i̲s̲c̲u̲s̲s̲i̲n̲g̲ that issue.

Guidelines for Choosing Verbals

In English, a verb can be followed by a verb form called a verbal. For example, in the sentence *He d̲e̲c̲i̲d̲e̲d̲ ̲t̲o̲ ̲g̲o̲ to the library,* the verb *decided* is followed by the verbal *to go*. A verbal following a verb may be an infinitive, a gerund, or occasionally a base form. There is no grammar rule, however, that will tell you which form of the verb will follow another verb. Some verbs are followed by a gerund, other verbs are followed by an infinitive, while still other verbs can be followed by either. Thus, you will need to learn, on a case-by-case basis, which verbal form should be used after a given verb.

Study these rules for adding verbals. Then study the list of commonly used verbs and the verbals that follow them.

1. **Some verbs must be followed by an infinitive.**

   Incorrect: Paul agreed g̲o̲i̲n̲g̲ to Sacramento tomorrow.

   Incorrect: Paul agreed g̲o̲ to Sacramento tomorrow.

   Correct: Paul agreed t̲o̲ ̲g̲o̲ to Sacramento tomorrow.

   Note: Some verbs, such as *ask, choose, want,* or *expect,* can be followed by a noun or pronoun before the infinitive. In the following example, the noun *Isabel* functions both as the direct object of *wants* and as the subject of the infinitive.

   Example: IBM wants Isabel t̲o̲ ̲f̲l̲y̲ to New York for an interview.

2. **Some verbs must be followed by a gerund.**

   Incorrect: Bill gave up t̲o̲ ̲s̲t̲u̲d̲y̲ for the exam.

   Incorrect: Bill gave up s̲t̲u̲d̲y̲ for the exam.

   Correct: Bill gave up s̲t̲u̲d̲y̲i̲n̲g̲ for the exam.

3. **Some verbs can be followed by either a gerund or an infinitive.**

   Incorrect: Mia likes s̲a̲i̲l̲ on Folsom Lake.

   Correct: Mia likes t̲o̲ ̲s̲a̲i̲l̲ on Folsom Lake.

   Correct: Mia likes s̲a̲i̲l̲i̲n̲g̲ on Folsom Lake.

4. A small commonly used group of verbs *(make, let, help, have)* must be followed by a base form (the infinitive without *to*). These verbs always have a noun or pronoun between them.

Incorrect: Please make the children <u>to go</u>^{vf} upstairs.

Incorrect: Please make the children <u>going</u>^{vf} upstairs.

Correct: Please make the children <u>go</u> upstairs.

Incorrect: Joseph let me <u>to carry</u>^{vf} his suitcase.

Correct: Joseph let me <u>carry</u> his suitcase.

Note: The verb *help* may be followed by either a base form or an infinitive.

Example: Hien helped the elderly woman <u>cross</u> the street.
           OR
           Hien helped the elderly woman <u>to cross</u> the street.

Commonly Used Verbs Followed by Infinitives, Gerunds, or Base Forms

● **Verbs Followed by an Infinitive:**

agree	endeavor	plan
appear	fail	prepare
attempt	hesitate	promise
consent	hope	refuse
decide	intend	seem
demand	need	tend
deserve	offer	volunteer
		wish

Examples: He hesitated <u>to call</u> me.
           She promised <u>to write</u> soon.
           We will attempt <u>to finish</u> the task by tomorrow.

Note: The following verbs **can** take a noun or pronoun before the infinitive.

ask	expect	prepare
beg	intend	promise
choose	need	want

Examples: I asked him <u>to go</u>.
           I need you <u>to help</u>.

Note: Except in the passive voice, the following verbs **must** have a noun or
pronoun before the infinitive.

advise	encourage	remind
allow	forbid	require
appoint	force	select
authorize	hire	teach
cause	instruct	tell
challenge	invite	tempt
command	order	trust
convince	permit	

Examples: He challenged me <u>to participate</u> in the contest.

I will remind you <u>to get up</u> early.

She was advised <u>to leave</u>. (passive voice)

- **Verbs Followed by a Gerund:**

admit	dislike	postpone	resent
avoid	enjoy	quit	resume
consider	finish	recall	risk
deny	imagine	recommend	suggest
discuss	miss	regret	

Examples: I miss <u>seeing</u> you.

Barbara cannot risk <u>going</u>.

- **Verbs Followed by Either a Gerund or an Infinitive:**

begin	prefer
continue	remember
hate	start
like	stop
love	try

Examples: I like <u>to hike</u>.

I like <u>hiking</u>.

- **Verbs Followed by a Base Form:**

make

have

let

help (This verb can also be followed by an infinitive.)

Examples: I will let you <u>know</u>.

Could you help me <u>carry</u> these boxes?

PROBLEM 4. The infinitive has been incorrectly formed.

Incorrect: It was hard for Naomi to admitted to her friends that she could not afford the high cost of college.

Correct: It was hard for Naomi <u>to admit</u> to her friends that she could not afford the high cost of college.

Incorrect: Mike often forgets <u>to checks</u> his mail on Saturdays.

Correct: Mike often forgets <u>to check</u> his mail on Saturdays.

Self–help Strategy: Remember that infinitives consist of *to* + base form, and nothing can be added to this base form. Do not add an *–ed* ending to the infinitive, even if the main verb of the sentence is in the past tense. Do not add an *–s* ending to an infinitive form either.

PROBLEM 5. The base form of a verb has been used instead of a gerund or an infinitive.

Incorrect: He says that <u>discuss</u> his problem would be too painful.

Correct: He says that <u>discussing</u> his problem would be too painful.

Correct: He says that <u>to discuss</u> his problem would be too painful.

Incorrect: <u>Study</u> all night does not always guarantee that a person will pass an exam.

Correct: <u>Studying</u> all night does not always guarantee that a person will pass an exam.

Incorrect: It is easy <u>communicate</u> with him.

Correct: It is easy <u>to communicate</u> with him.

Incorrect: He changed his way of <u>look</u> at them.

Correct: He changed his way of <u>looking</u> at them.

Incorrect: By <u>study</u>, we can learn these formulas.

Correct: By <u>studying</u>, we can learn these formulas.

Guidelines for Using Gerunds and Infinitives

The rules for using gerunds and infinitives in the positions illustrated in the previous sentences are complex and will not be treated in detail in this text. If you want to know a particular rule in more detail, you may wish to consult an advanced ESL grammar book. You will, however, find the following guidelines useful.

1. **Avoid using the base form when a verbal functions as a subject or an object.**

   Examples: <u>To win</u> (not *win*) the election is what he wants.

   <u>Reading</u> (not *read*) is one of her hobbies.

   We have benefited greatly from <u>listening</u> (not *listen*) to her lectures.

2. **Gerunds, not base forms, are used as objects of prepositions.**

    Examples: Pedro helped me by <u>coming</u> over to visit.

    Martha talked me into <u>helping</u> her.

3. **Infinitives are used after certain adjectives.**

    Examples: I am sorry <u>to see</u> you so unhappy.

    I am eager <u>to get</u> my B.S. degree.

4. **Infinitives are used to express a purpose.**

    Example: He went to the TA's office <u>to ask</u> a question. (The *to* is a shortened form of *in order to*.)

PROBLEM 6. A [verb + preposition] problem has occurred.

a. **A preposition that goes with a verb is missing.**

   Note: Your instructor may mark verb-form errors of this type as follows: **vf (+ prep)**

   Incorrect: I will have to study more tonight <u>to compensate</u> the time I lost yesterday. *vf (+ prep)*

   Correct: I will have to study more tonight <u>to compensate for</u> the time I lost yesterday.

   Incorrect: The two teams will <u>compete</u> each other next week. *vf (+ prep)*

   Correct: The two teams will <u>compete with</u> each other next week.

   (**Note**: *compete against* is also correct.)

b. **A preposition is used when it is not needed after a specific verb.**

   Note: Your instructor may mark verb-form errors of this type as follows: **vf (no prep)**

   Incorrect: In my paper, I <u>emphasized about</u> the need for smaller classes for undergraduates. *vf (no prep)*

   Correct: In my paper, I <u>emphasized</u> the need for smaller classes for undergraduates.

   Incorrect: The reporter got her information by <u>interviewing with</u> three people. *vf (no prep)*

   Correct: The reporter got her information by <u>interviewing</u> three people.

c. **The wrong preposition has been used.**

   Note: Your instructor may mark verb-form errors of this type a follows: **vf (wrong prep)**

   Incorrect: The professor often <u>refers on</u> the textbook. *vf (wrong prep)*

   Correct: The professor often <u>refers to</u> the textbook.

vf (wrong prep)
Incorrect: In the spring, Mike often <u>suffers of</u> allergies.
Correct: In the spring, Mike often <u>suffers from</u> allergies.

Self-help Strategy: If you want to know whether a certain verb needs an accompanying preposition, check the verb in an ESL dictionary.

d. A preposition that is part of a phrasal verb (two-word or three-word verb) is incorrect or missing.

vf (wrong prep)
Incorrect: He just <u>hung off</u> the phone.
Correct: He just <u>hung up</u> the phone.

vf (wrong prep)
Incorrect: We will have to <u>call over</u> the birthday party.
Correct: We will have to <u>call off</u> the birthday party.

vf (+ prep)
Incorrect: I am going to have to work hard to <u>catch up</u> the work that I have missed.
Correct: I am going to have to work hard to <u>catch up on</u> the work that I have missed.

Self-help Strategy: Although phrasal verbs are used more frequently in speaking than in writing, they are also used in written English. Thus, you will want to be aware of them. These two- and three-word verbs sometimes, but not always, have a more formal one-word synonym that you can use in written English. For example, in the sentence *We had to call off the party, call off* has the same meaning as *cancel.* In the sentence *Could you turn down the volume, turn down* has the same meaning as *decrease.* These phrasal verbs are highly complex in that a preposition (sometimes called a **particle** when part of a phrasal verb) can completely change the meaning of the verb. Read the following examples and note how the meaning changes:

Please <u>turn on</u> the light. (meaning = start the operation of)
Please <u>turn in</u> the assignment on Friday. (meaning = submit)
I usually <u>turn over</u> a lot when I sleep. (meaning = turn from one side to the other)

Another complexity is that some phrasal verbs have more than one meaning depending on the context.

Please <u>turn down</u> the volume. (meaning = decrease)
I hope you will not <u>turn down</u> the job even though the pay is not what you had hoped for. (meaning = refuse)
Five thousand people <u>turned out</u> to hear the concert. (meaning = came)
Please <u>turn out</u> the light. (meaning = extinguish)

The best way to learn these two- and three-word verbs is to listen for them in conversations and to look for them in written material. They are also listed in ESL dictionaries.

■ PART III: Exercises

> ### In Part III, you will practice
>
> • *recognizing and correcting verb-form errors in sentences*
> • *using verb forms correctly in sentences and in a paragraph*
> • *using prepositions that accompany certain verbs*
> • *identifying and correcting verb-form errors in a paragraph*

EXERCISE I (Do this exercise on your own. Then check your answers with a classmate.)

Directions: Examine each verb form in the following sentences to decide whether a sentence is correct (C) or incorrect (I). Then cross out each incorrect verb form and write the correct form above it.

> Example: _I_ Everyone should know where he or she ~~are came~~ *comes* from.

_____1. I have live in the United States for two years.

_____2. Juan has just withdrawn some money from his bank account.

_____3. By exercise on a regular basis, an athlete can build a strong body, maintain muscle flexibility, and develop stamina.

_____4. In the case of my younger sister, punishment seems to be an effective way to make her behaving better.

_____5. If I can succeed in college and went to medical school, I will have the opportunity to pursue the career I want.

_____6. My instructor does not please with my lack of participation in class.

_____7. I believe that I have a good chance of get into medical school.

_____8. Scientists are currently try to find a cure for AIDS.

_____9. Elizabeth has decided to postpone taking the GRE until next summer.

_____10. I did not expected you to call me so soon.

_____11. I have been wearing my favorite jeans so much that they are becoming rather worn over.

_____12. By the time I got home, my roommate had already cook, even though it was my turn to make dinner.

_____13. I talked my roommate into helping me with my math homework.

_____14. My best friend asked me to take a vacation and to came to California for a visit.

EXERCISE 2 (Do this exercise on your own. Then check your answers with a classmate.)

Directions: Fill in each blank with the correct form (gerund, infinitive, or base form) of a verb of your choice. Use a verb form even if other parts of speech are possible. If necessary, add words in addition to the verb to complete the sentence grammatically.

Example: Jack plans _to go_ to the movies tonight after he finishes _studying_ .

---

1. I avoided _____ my friend last night because I am angry at him.

2. Many students prefer _____ late at night rather than during the day.

3. By _____ , we can work out our problems.

4. These boxes are too heavy for me. Could you help me _____ them?

5. The coach encouraged the team _____ .

6. One of my goals is _____ .

7. Many students dislike _____ .

8. _____ is one of my hobbies.

9. I am good at _____ .

10. A classmate let me _____ his notes when I was not able to come to class last week.

11. It is easy _____ there by train.

EXERCISE 3 (Do this exercise on your own. Then check your answers with a classmate.)

Directions: Check your knowledge of prepositions that accompany common verbs by filling in each blank with the correct preposition.

Example: My brother is upset because he has been accused _of_ lying.

---

1. My neighbors make so much noise that I have trouble concentrating _____ my work .

2. I dreamed _____ you last night.

3. I don't know if I can ever forgive you _____ lying to me.

4. Are you interested _____ going camping with us next weekend?

5. My advisor insisted _____ my submitting a research proposal by January.

6. I will have to think _____ what you have said before I give you an answer.

7. I am hopeful that I will succeed _____ finishing my B.S. by next year.

8. My parents don't object _____ my borrowing their car on weekends.

9. We want to take advantage _____ the nice weather and go on a picnic.

EXERCISE 4 (Do this exercise on your own. Then check your answers with a classmate.)

Directions: Fill in each blank space with the correct form of the verb in parentheses.

One of my very favorite activities is _to walk/walking_ (walk) through

the arboretum near my dormitory. After a stressful day of classes, I go

there _____ (relax) and _____ (enjoy) the sight

and smell of the trees. As I _____ (stroll) along the path next

to a small creek, I pass numerous tall trees including redwoods, oaks,

and pines. I also pass a lake with ducks on it. The natural beauty and

quiet of the area helps me _____ (relax). I enjoy _____

(walk) through the arboretum any time of the year, but on a hot summer

day, it is especially refreshing. The shade from the trees keeps the area cool no matter how hot it is. I am always refreshed and ready

_____ (continue) studying after a walk through the arboretum.

EXERCISE 5 (Do this exercise on your own. Then check your answers with a classmate.)

Directions: The following paragraph, written by a student, has been edited so that the only errors are in verb form. Test your knowledge of verb forms by finding and correcting the verb-form errors in this paragraph. Cross out each incorrect form and write the correct form above it.

It takes a great deal of courage for a person to leave his or her family
start
and ~~starts~~ life all over again in another country. The person not only

must face many changes alone but also must separate from friends and

rely on letters as a means of share thoughts. The new environment and

the new setting make even the bravest individual feels scared, as he or

she encounters many sudden changes and undergo many kinds of strug-

gles in a short period of time. Despite these difficulties, go abroad as an

immigrant has many benefits. To go abroad gives a person the chance to

see the world, to face new challenges, to make new friends, and gaining

more knowledge about people and places. Before I came to the United

States, I had many expectations. I thought that life in this country would

be similar to life in my country. However, after being here for five

months, I have came to the conclusion that life in the United States is

entirely different from what I had expect.

EXERCISE 6 (Do this exercise on your own.)

Directions: Choose a short article in a newspaper or magazine. After reading the article, underline all the verb forms in two paragraphs. Can you understand why the different verb forms are used? If you are unsure of any of them,
ask a classmate, a tutor, or your instructor.

■ PART IV: Writing Activity

> ### In Part IV, you will
> - *plan and write a response to a selected topic*
> - *share your writing with a classmate*
> - *edit your writing for content and sentence-level accuracy*

Step 1—Choosing a Writing Topic

Select one or both of the following:

Topic A: Discuss one of your goals. It may be either an immediate goal or a long-term goal. Explain what this goal is and why you want to accomplish it.

Topic B: Explain how to do something. First, introduce the activity. Then explain the process of how to do it, step by step.

Step 2—Gathering Information

Once you have selected a topic, discuss it with a classmate or in a small group. If you have chosen Topic A, share one or more goals that each person has. Discuss why you each have these goals. If you have chosen Topic B, each of you should explain the process of doing something. Make sure the steps are clear to the others in your group.

Step 3—Prewriting

Working by yourself, list some of the ideas you have discussed with a classmate or in a small group. For Topic A, write down several goals and why you want to accomplish them. Identify one that you are particularly interested in writing about. For Topic B, jot down the steps in the process you have chosen to explain.

Step 4—Writing Your First Draft

Use your notes to write your draft. Focus on content.

Step 5—Sharing Your Draft

Working with a classmate, read each other's draft. Give feedback to each other using the following format.

A. Reading for Content

1. What did you like most about this paper?
2. What would you like to know more about?
3. What suggestions do you have for the writer?

B. Checking for Errors in Verb Form

1. Circle any verb-form errors you notice in your classmate's draft.

2. Discuss how to correct them.

Step 6—Revising Your Writing

Using your classmate's suggestions as well as your own ideas for revising, write your second draft. Focus on content and sentence-level accuracy, and pay special attention to verb forms.

Step 7—Proofreading Your Final Draft

Read your final draft once again, paying particular attention to verb-form errors. Make any necessary changes.

Postwriting Activity

Step 1—When your paper is returned, check to see if your instructor has marked any verb-form errors.

Step 2—If so, review the material in *Part II* of this unit.

Step 3—Correct each verb-form error by rewriting the sentence that contains the error. If you are unsure of a correction, ask your instructor or a classmate for help.

■ PART V: Applying What You Have Learned to Other Writing Assignments

In Part V, you will

* *look for and correct verb-form errors in writing assignments you have already completed*

If you are in a composition class or another class in which you do written assignments, take your last returned paper and follow these directions:

1. Check whether your instructor has marked any verb-form errors. If so, try to correct them, using the material you have learned in this unit.

2. If your instructor has not marked any verb-form errors, take one paragraph and underline each verb. Determine whether each verb is correct in form.

3. When you are writing in the future, check for accuracy in verb form.

UNIT 3:
MODALS*

*modal = grading symbol for modal errors

■ PART I: What You Need to Know About Modal Errors

> ### *In Part I, you will answer the following questions:*
> * *What is a modal error?*
> * *Why is it important to avoid errors with modals in writing?*
> * *What are some strategies for mastering modals?*

Definition of the Error

Modals are auxiliaries, such as *may*, *might*, *should*, *must*, *can*, and *could*, that add specific meanings to verbs. In the sentences below, notice how the modal adds a specific meaning to the verb *exercise*.

> I <u>exercise</u> at the gym regularly. (a fact)
> a. I <u>might exercise</u> at the gym tonight. (a possibility)
> b. I <u>should exercise</u> at the gym more often. (advice to myself)
> c. I <u>could have exercised</u> at the gym yesterday. (an opportunity that I did not take advantage of)

A modal error (**modal**) is an error involving the wrong choice of a modal, the wrong form of any part of a modal verb phrase, or the wrong time reference of a modal verb phrase. A modal verb phrase consists of a modal and all the verbs that appear with it, including the main verb.

Importance of Mastering Modals in Writing

Errors with modals involve verbs and are thus global (more serious) errors that can affect the meaning of a text considerably. Moreover, writers who are not able to use modals in their writing will have limited ability to show the difference between facts, inferences, and possibilities in English, a distinction frequently made in academic writing.

The following examples illustrate how modals can be used to show inferences and possibilities:

Example 1: Someone I know has lived in the dorm for four years. (a known fact)

Because most students stay in the dorm for only one or two years, the person I know <u>must like</u> the dorm very much. (a logical inference based on the above fact)

Example 2: My roommate did not eat much at dinner last night. (a known fact)

She <u>might be trying</u> to lose weight. OR She <u>might not have been</u> very hungry. (logical inferences marked as possibilities by the modal *might*)

As you can see, being able to use modals increases your ability to express your ideas clearly and concisely.

Suggestions for Mastering Modals

To master the use of modals, you will need to study the functions of the different modals. You will also want to learn the forms of the modals and the time references expressed by these forms. You can use the chart in this unit to help you. If you need further explanation, you can look up modals in an intermediate or advanced ESL grammar book.

You can also become aware of the use of modals in what you read. As you read books, articles, and other material, focus on how writers use modals to add meaning to verbs in English.

TEST YOUR UNDERSTANDING OF MODALS

After you have read *Part I*, write answers to the following questions. Share your answers with another student.

1. What is a modal? Explain in your own words.
2. How serious are modal errors? Explain your answer.
3. How can using modals help you when you write in English?
4. Evaluate your own use of modals. Do you use them effectively and accurately?
5. What strategies can you use to avoid modal errors? These strategies may be from this section or from your own thinking.

■ PART II: Common Problems, Rules, and Self-help Strategies

In Part II, you will

- *study three problems ESL writers commonly have with modals*
- *review selected rules that will help you use modals correctly*
- *study a chart that gives the functions and forms of modals*

This section presents three problems ESL writers commonly have with modals. First, study each problem and the examples that illustrate it. Then mark the problems you think you have when you write in English. Remember that if you become aware of the type of modal errors you most often make, you will increase your chances of avoiding these errors in your writing.

PROBLEM 1. The wrong modal has been chosen to express the writer's intended meaning.

Incorrect: I <u>must have gone</u> to see my instructor during office hours, but I
did not have time.
modal

Correct: I <u>should have gone</u> to see my instructor during office hours, but
I did not have time.

PROBLEM 2. The modal verb phrase has been incorrectly formed.

Note: Your instructor may mark this kind of modal error **modal (vf)** to
indicate that the error is a modal verb-form error.

Incorrect: She <u>might studies</u> in the library tonight.
modal (vf)

Incorrect: She <u>might to study</u> in the library tonight.
modal (vf)

Correct: She <u>might study</u> in the library tonight.

Incorrect: I <u>should had studied</u> last night.
modal (vf)

Correct: I <u>should have studied</u> last night.

PROBLEM 3. The time reference of the modal verb phrase is incorrect.

> *Note*: Your instructor may mark this kind of modal error **modal (vt)** to indicate that the error is a modal verb-tense error.
>
> Incorrect: My muscles are sore. I <u>should not exercise</u> so hard yesterday. *modal (vt)*
>
> Correct: My muscles are sore. I <u>should not have exercised</u> so hard yesterday.

Guide to Forming Modals

Present Time

a. modal + base form (infinitive without *to*)

> Example: What does he usually do for exercise?
>
> He <u>might exercise</u> at the gym, but I do not know for sure.
>
> (Time = present habitual)

b. modal + be + present participle (*-ing* form)

> Example: What is he doing right now?
>
> He <u>might be exercising</u> at the gym.
>
> (Time = right now)

Future Time

a. modal + base form (infinitive without *to*)

> Example: What is she going to do tomorrow night?
>
> She <u>might exercise</u> at the gym.
>
> (Time = future)

Past Time

a. modal + have + past participle

> Example: What did he do last night?
>
> He <u>might have exercised</u> at the gym.
>
> (Time = past)

b. modal + have + been + present participle

> Example: What was he doing when you called last night?
>
> He <u>might have been exercising</u> at the gym.
>
> (Time = past)

Note: Do not forget the *to* in *ought to* and *have to*.

Examples: We <u>ought to</u> study before the test.
We <u>have to</u> study before the test.
We <u>ought to</u> have studied more than we did.
We <u>had to</u> study hard before the test.

Functions and Forms of Modals: How to Use the Chart

For your reference, a chart of the modals is provided on the following pages. In the left-hand column, you will find each modal listed. In the second column, you will see the functions most commonly expressed by each modal—that is, the meanings that each modal adds to a verb. Note that some modals have more than one function. For example, *must* expresses necessity as in the sentence *I must leave immediately* or probability/assumption as in the sentence *You have been working long hours. You must be busy.*

In the third column, you will find example sentences illustrating the functions of each modal in the present/future time frame, while in the fourth column, you will find example sentences for each modal used in the past time frame. Study the third and fourth columns not only to understand what the modals mean but also to learn how to form each modal in the present and past. Note, for example, that the past of *can* is *could* (as in *I could do ten push-ups five years ago, but now I cannot.*), while the past of *could* (meaning possibility) is *could have* + past participle (as in *Mary could have been at the party, although I didn't see her.*). In particular, note that the modal *must* has two different past forms, each of which expresses a different meaning. For example, the past of the sentence *I must go* is *I had to go*. Here the modal *must* expresses necessity. On the other hand, the past of the sentence *You must be busy* is *You must have been busy*. Here, in contrast, the modal *must* implies probability/assumption.

If you have difficulty using the modals correctly, study the chart in detail. If, on the other hand, you find that you are occasionally unsure of the function or form of a modal, use the chart for handy reference.

FUNCTIONS AND FORMS OF MODALS

Modal	Function	Form in Present/Future	Form in Past
can	To show ability	I <u>can run</u> ten miles.	I <u>could run</u> ten miles when I was in high school.
	To suggest a possibility or to give an option	Students <u>can pre-enroll</u> in classes or sign up at in-person registration.	
	To ask for or to give permission	<u>Can</u> I <u>call</u> you? You <u>can leave</u> when you have finished your exam.	
	To show impossibility	It <u>cannot be</u> Jim standing over there. He went away for the weekend.	
could	To show past ability		I <u>could run</u> ten miles when I was in high school.
	To ask a polite question	<u>Could</u> I call you?	
	To show possibility	Why isn't Maria here? She <u>could be</u> busy.	Why wasn't Maria at the party last night? She <u>could have been</u> busy.
	To show impossibility	He <u>could not be</u> here at the party. He is out of town.	He <u>could not have been</u> at the party last night. He was out of town.

Modal	Function	Form in Present/Future	Form in Past
could (*cont.*)	To suggest a possibility or to give an option	You <u>could try</u> going to Doctor Davidson to see if she can help you with your back problem.	
	To show a past opportunity that was not realized		I <u>could have asked</u> for help on the last math problem set, but I was determined to do it myself.
may	To ask for or to give permission (formal)	<u>May</u> I <u>call</u> you? You <u>may leave</u> when you have finished your exam.	
	To show possibility	The instructor <u>may come</u> to class late today.	The instructor <u>may have come</u> to class late yesterday.
might	To show possibility	The instructor <u>might come</u> to class late today.	The instructor <u>might have come</u> to class late yesterday.
should	To show advisability	You <u>should try</u> that new restaurant downtown. It is excellent.	
	To show advisability after the fact		We <u>should have tried</u> that new restaurant downtown. (But we did not.) You <u>should not have said</u> that to Tom. (But you did.)

Modal	Function	Form in Present/Future	Form in Past
should (*cont.*)	**To show obligation**	I <u>should renew</u> my driver's license. It expires next month.	
	To show an obligation that was not carried out		I <u>should have renewed</u> my driver's license (But I forgot to do so.)
	To show expectation	You <u>should receive</u> my letter in two days.	
	To show an expectation that was not realized		You <u>should have received</u> my letter two days ago. (But you did not.)
ought to	**To show advisability**	Everyone <u>ought to</u> exercise regularly.	
	To show advisability after the fact		Francis <u>ought to have exercised</u> before his backpacking trip. (But he didn't.)
	To show obligation	I <u>ought to register</u> to vote if I want to vote in the next election.	
	To show an obligation that was not carried out		I <u>ought to have registered</u> to vote by October 5. (But I did not register.)

Modal	Function	Form in Present/Future	Form in Past
ought to (*cont.*)	**To show expectation**	You <u>ought to receive</u> my letter in two days.	
	To show an expectation that was not realized		You <u>ought to have received</u> my letter two days ago. (But you did not.)
had better	**To show advisability**	We <u>had better leave</u>. It is getting late.	
must	**To show probability or to make a logical assumption**	Janice <u>must be</u> out this evening. She does not answer her telephone.	Janice <u>must have been</u> out last night She did not answer her telephone.
	To show necessity	I <u>must call</u> my parents tonight. I have not talked with them in a long time.	I was late for the meeting because I <u>had to call</u> my parents last night.
	To show prohibition	You <u>must not smoke</u> in the classroom at any time. We <u>mustn't forget</u> to call Bill and Teresa tonight.	
have to	**To show necessity**	Mike <u>has to make up</u> the physics lab he missed.	Mike <u>had to make up</u> the physics lab he missed.
	To show lack of necessity	I am glad that I <u>do not have to cook</u> tonight.	I <u>did not have to cook</u> last night.

Modal	Function	Form in Present/Future	Form in Past
will	**To indicate future time**	We <u>will leave</u> for the airport at 7:00 A.M. tomorrow.	
	To make a promise or to show willingness	The federal government <u>will provide</u> assistance to the hurricane victims.	
	To state a general truth	The new car they have developed <u>will run</u> on either gasoline or ethanol. (*Note:* time = present)	
	To ask a polite question	Mike, <u>will</u> you <u>help</u> me with these heavy boxes? I cannot lift them myself. (*Note:* time = right now)	
would	**To ask a polite question**	<u>Would</u> you please <u>call</u> me later tonight?	
	To indicate a repeated action in the past		When I lived in Los Angeles, I <u>would go</u> to the beach every weekend.
	To indicate future time in a sentence that is in the past		Mark promised that he <u>would help</u> me with my math homework. I did not realize how much I <u>would like</u> my new apartment.

Modal	Function	Form in Present/Future	Form in Past
would rather	**To show a preference**	I <u>would rather go</u> to summer school than graduate late.	
would like	**To express a desire**	I <u>would like to go</u> to medical school.	
	To express a desire that was not realized		I <u>would have liked</u> to have gone (OR to go) to medical school. (But I did not.)

■ PART III: Exercises

> ### In Part III, you will practice
> - *distinguishing between the present and past forms of modals*
> - *understanding the meaning of the modals*
> - *recognizing and correcting modal errors in individual sentences*
> - *recognizing modals and understanding their meaning in a text*
> - *using modals correctly in a paragraph*

EXERCISE 1 (Do this exercise on your own. Then check your answers with a classmate.)

Directions: To practice distinguishing between the present and past forms of modals, change the following sentences from present to past time. For some of the sentences, you will also need to change time words and phrases. Refer to the modals chart to ensure that you have chosen the correct past forms.

Example: I do not see Monica at the reception, but she might arrive later.

Past: *I did not see Monica at the reception, but she might have arrived later.*

---

1. Bob might be joking about his decision to quit school.

   Past: _____

   _____

2. Lian could be joking about her poor handwriting skills.

   Past: _____

   _____

3. Max, who is on the track team, can run a mile in 4 minutes, 30 seconds.

   Past: When he was on the track team, Max _____

   _____

4. Jill must be tired after working ten hours today.

   Past: _____

   _____

5. Because Lydia needs to get a good grade on her chemistry midterm, she must study this evening.

   Past: _____

   _____

6. I should exercise more often.

   Past: _____

   _____

7. You ought to send your roommate's parents a thank-you note when you get home.

   Past: _____

   _____

8. My supervisor must be sick since she did not attend the office barbeque this afternoon.

   Past: _____

   _____

9. Mary may not have time to call her parents tonight.

   Past: _____

   _____

10. My roommate has to do the shopping this week.

    Past: _____

    _____

EXERCISE 2 (Do this exercise on your own. Then check your answers with a classmate.)

Directions: Use a modal to express the underlined part of each of the following ideas. Note that by using a modal, you can often make your writing less wordy.

Example: I didn't see Bob at the library. <u>It's possible that I missed him.</u>
I might have missed him.

---

1. I didn't see Judy at the library after 10 P.M. <u>She probably left early.</u>

   _____

   _____

2. The sky is getting cloudy. <u>There is a chance of rain.</u>

   _____

   _____

3. Elena didn't come to class yesterday. <u>It was necessary for her to go to Sacramento.</u>

   _____

   _____

4. Linda received a gift from her aunt. <u>It would be a good idea for her to send a thank-you note.</u>

   _____

   _____

5. We don't have much work to do today. <u>It is possible that our supervisor will allow us to leave early.</u>

   _____

   _____

6. My brother–in–law just bought a nice house in an expensive section of town. <u>I assume the house cost a lot of money.</u>

   _____

   _____

7. José was available to help over the weekend. <u>In retrospect, I realize that it would have been a good idea to have asked him to help.</u>

_____

_____

8. When I was young, <u>I knew how to speak French</u>, but I have forgotten it since I never use it.

_____

_____

9. <u>My housemate had time to wash the dishes last night</u>, but she went out instead.

_____

_____

10. <u>One possibility or option that we have is to camp out</u> on our way to the Grand Canyon.

_____

_____

EXERCISE 3 (Do this exercise on your own. Then check your answers with a classmate.)

Directions: Some of the following sentences contain errors in the use of modals. First, decide if a sentence is correct (C) or incorrect (I). If it is incorrect, cross out the incorrect form and write the correction above. Be able to explain to a classmate the meaning that the modal gives to the verb.

Example: ___I___ I shouldn't ~~had~~ *have* told you about my problem because now you are worried.

_____1. My brother must had forgotten to call me.

_____2. My brother could have call me while I was at the library.

_____3. My brother may calls late tonight.

_____4. I did not have time to stop at the store because I must have stayed late at the office to finish my work.

_____5. Susan felt she could have worked out longer in the gym, but her coach advised her not to do so.

_____6. I got a speeding ticket! I should not have be driving over the speed limit on the freeway.

_____7. My roommate is in Hawaii applying for a job. It should be warm there even though it's winter here.

_____8. Most people now realize that we must take action soon to save the environment.

EXERCISE 4 (Do this exercise with a classmate.)

Directions: Underline each modal or modal verb phrase in the following paragraph. Then discuss with a classmate the meaning each modal gives to the sentence that contains it.

Grand Canyon National Park in Arizona is a paradise for nature lovers and outdoor enthusiasts. Visitors will be awed by the fabulous view of the canyon, its vast depth, and beautifully colored walls. The National Park Headquarters and Visitor Center is at the South Rim where visitors can pick up information about the park. Visitors who have only a little time to spend can view the canyon from either the North Rim or the South Rim. People who have more time may want to see more of the Grand Canyon than just the North or South Rim. Visitors can drive along parts of the rim or hike down into the canyon on various trails. In fact, hikers can walk or ride a mule all the way to the bottom of the canyon to the Colorado River. However, hikers must be sure to drink plenty of water to avoid dehydration as the weather can be extremely hot and dry. At the bottom, hikers can stay at either Phantom Ranch, which consists of cabins and dormitories, or an adjacent campground. Perhaps the best way to see the canyon, however, is to float down the Colorado

River either on a rubber raft or in a wooden dory. Seeing the canyon from this perspective is spectacular, but people who are afraid of big whitewater should not take this trip since some of the Colorado River rapids are among the biggest in the world. For most visitors, a trip to the Grand Canyon should be a truly unforgettable experience.

EXERCISE 5   (Do this exercise on your own. Then check your answers with a classmate.)

Directions: Fill in each blank with the correct modal verb phrase. The main verb and modal meaning are indicated in parentheses. The first blank has been filled in as an example.

Writing a term paper last semester was very challenging for me. At the beginning of the term, I was looking forward to doing the research and writing the paper. But, unfortunately, I waited longer than I *should have waited* (wait/**advisability**) to get started. I _____ (start/**opportunity**) earlier, but for some reason I just kept waiting. I found myself working right up until the last minute. I know I _____ (proofread/**advisability**) the paper more carefully. I also _____ (add/**opportunity**) some illustrations if I had had more time. Because I started so late, not only did I have to submit a less than satisfactory paper, but I also _____ (stay up/**necessity**) all night to finish it.

EXERCISE 6   (Do this exercise on your own.)

Directions: Choose a short article in a newspaper or a magazine. Read the article, checking to see whether any modals have been used. If so, underline them and identify the meaning they give to the sentence.

■ PART IV: Writing Activity

In Part IV, you will
- *plan and write a response to a selected topic*
- *share your writing with a classmate*
- *edit your writing for content and sentence-level accuracy*

Step 1—Choosing a Writing Topic

Select one or more of the following:

Topic A: Write about what you see as one of the most serious problems facing the world today. First, explain what the problem is. Then, discuss what you think can and should be done to try to solve it.

Topic B: Write about a situation that you feel you did not handle as well as you could have. First, explain the situation. Then discuss what you could have done differently.

Topic C: Advise someone on how to be a successful student. What should a student do to be successful? If you are working, you may want to give advice on how to be successful in your line of work.

Step 2—Gathering Information

With a classmate or in a small group discuss the topic you have selected. If you have chosen Topic A, discuss some of the most serious problems facing the world today. What do you think can and should be done about them? If you have chosen Topic B, discuss a situation you did not handle as well as you could have. What could you have done differently? If you have chosen Topic C, discuss the advice you would give to someone on how to be a successful student.

Step 3—Prewriting

Working by yourself, list some of the ideas you have discussed with a classmate or in a small group. For Topic A, make notes on the problems you have discussed and decide which one is the most serious. Then jot down notes on ways you think this problem could or should be handled. For Topic B, list some of the ideas you have for what you could have done differently in the situation you have chosen to write about. For Topic C, list the advice you would give to someone on how to be a successful student.

Step 4—Writing Your First Draft

Using your notes from prewriting, write your first draft. Focus on content.

Step 5—Sharing Your Draft

Working with a classmate, read each other's draft. Give feedback to each other by answering these questions:

A. Reading for Content
1. What do you like about this draft?
2. What would you still like to know more about?
3. What suggestions do you have for the writer?

B. Checking for Errors with Modals
1. Circle any errors with modals you notice in your classmate's draft.
2. Discuss how to correct them.

Step 6—Revising Your Writing

Using your classmate's suggestions as well as your own ideas for revising, write your second draft. Focus on content and sentence-level accuracy. As you check each sentence, be especially aware of any errors with modals.

Step 7—Proofreading Your Final Draft

Read your final draft once again, paying particular attention to modals. Make any necessary changes.

Postwriting Activity

Step 1—When your writing is returned, check to see if your instructor has marked any errors with modals.

Step 2—If so, review the material in *Part II* of this unit.

Step 3—Correct each modal error by rewriting the sentence that contains the error. If you are unsure of a correction, ask your instructor or a classmate for help.

■ PART V: Applying What You Have Learned to Other Writing Assignments

In Part V, you will

• *look for and correct modal errors in any other writing assignments you have done*

If you are in a composition class or another class in which you do writing assignments, take your last returned paper and follow these directions:

1. Check whether your instructor has marked any modal errors on your paper. If so, correct them, using the material you have learned in this unit as a guide.

2. If your instructor has not marked any modal errors on your paper, read through the paper and underline any modals. Try to determine whether they are correctly used. If you are not sure, ask a classmate or your instructor to help you.

3. When you do writing assignments in the future, be aware of your use of modals and check for possible modal errors.

UNIT 4: CONDITIONAL*

*cond = grading symbol for conditional errors

■ PART I: What You Need to Know About Errors with Conditional Sentences

> ### In Part I, you will answer the following questions:
> - *What is an error with a conditional sentence?*
> - *Why is it important to avoid errors with conditional sentences in writing?*
> - *What are some strategies for mastering conditional sentences?*

Definition of the Error

A conditional sentence usually consists of an *if* clause that states a condition and a result clause that shows the effect of the condition. An example of a conditional sentence is *If I had time* (the condition), *I would go jogging* (the result). An error with a conditional sentence (**cond**) occurs when a conditional sentence has been incorrectly formed or has not been used where it is needed.

Conditional sentences can express two types of conditions: real and hypothetical (sometimes called unreal). Examples of these two types of conditional sentences follow. A full explanation of the two types of conditional sentences is given in *Part II*.

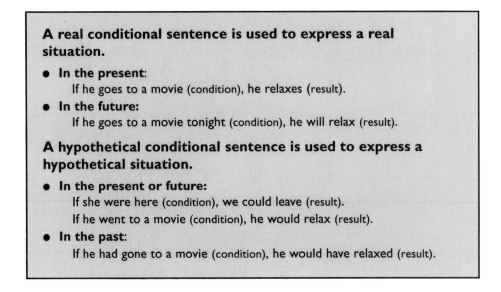

A real conditional sentence is used to express a real situation.

- **In the present:**
    If he goes to a movie (condition), he relaxes (result).
- **In the future:**
    If he goes to a movie tonight (condition), he will relax (result).

A hypothetical conditional sentence is used to express a hypothetical situation.

- **In the present or future:**
    If she were here (condition), we could leave (result).
    If he went to a movie (condition), he would relax (result).
- **In the past:**
    If he had gone to a movie (condition), he would have relaxed (result).

Importance of Mastering Conditional Sentences in Writing

Errors with conditional sentences are global and will affect the meaning of individual sentences, parts of a paragraph, and whole paragraphs. ESL writers can increase their ability to analyze in English by being able to control conditional sentences. Writers, for example, use conditional sentences to show cause-effect relationships (*If enrollment goes up* [condition], *classes become overcrowded* [result]); to speculate about a past event (*If I had studied the right chapters* [condition], *I would have at least received a B on my quiz* [result]); or to show a future possibility (*If the teacher lets class out early* [condition], *I will help you finish your calculus problems* [result]). Thus, to be able to show such relationships, ESL writers need to master conditional sentences.

Suggestions for Mastering Conditional Sentences

It is essential that you learn the correct formation of the verb phrase for both the *if* clause (the condition) and the result clause of a conditional sentence. When you revise, check **both** clauses to make sure that the verb phrase is correct in each one.

If you carefully listen for conditional sentences and look for them in your reading, you can increase your ability to use them in your own writing.

TEST YOUR KNOWLEDGE OF THE CONDITIONAL

After you have read *Part I*, write answers to the following questions. Share your answers with another student.

1. What is a conditional sentence? Define and give an example.
2. How serious are errors with the conditional? Explain your answer.
3. How do you express the conditional in your language?
4. How much and in what circumstances do you use the conditional when you write in English?
5. Why is it important for a writer to be able to control the conditional?

■ PART II: Common Problems, Rules, and Self-help Strategies

> **In Part II, you will**
> - study five problems ESL writers commonly have with conditional sentences
> - learn selected rules and self-help strategies for controlling errors with the conditional
> - study the meaning and use of different conditional sentences
> - learn how to form conditional verb phrases

This section presents five problems ESL writers commonly have with conditional sentences. First, study each problem and the examples that illustrate it. Then mark the problems you think you have when you write in English. Remember that if you become aware of the type of errors you most often make with conditional sentences, you will increase your chances of avoiding these errors in your writing.

PROBLEM 1. A conditional sentence has not been used where one is needed.

Incorrect: I know about the reading assignment. I would have done it.

Correct: If I had known about the reading assignment (condition), I would have done it (result).

Incorrect: Especially Peter does not have a new job before quitting his old job, he might have a hard time finding a job in the future.

Correct: If Peter does not have a new job before quitting his old job (condition), he might have a hard time finding a job in the future (result).

Self-help Strategy: When you are writing, keep in mind that if you want to show a condition and a result, you should use a conditional sentence.

PROBLEM 2. The wrong verb or verb phrase has been used in one of the clauses of a conditional sentence.

Incorrect: If I study hard for my anthropology midterm, I would pass it.

Correct: If I study hard for my anthropology midterm, I will pass it.

Correct: If I studied hard for my anthropology midterm, I would pass it.

Self-help Strategy: Always check to make sure you form the verb phrase correctly in **both** clauses of a conditional sentence. If you are unsure about which forms to use, consult the section on forming conditional verb phrases in this unit.

PROBLEM 3. A hypothetical conditional sentence has not been used where one is needed.

Incorrect: I am a very disorganized person. For instance, I often cannot find my English homework because I have put it in my math notebook. If I <u>am</u> more organized (condition), I <u>will have</u> separate color-coded folders for each class (result).

Correct: I am a very disorganized person. For instance, I often cannot find my English homework because I have put it in my math notebook. If I <u>were</u> more organized (condition), I <u>would have</u> separate color-coded folders for each class (result). (The writer is referring to a hypothetical situation, not a real situation.)

Self-help Strategy: Remember that the verbs you use in a conditional sentence show whether you are referring to a real or hypothetical situation. The past tense and the past perfect tense in the *if* clause of a conditional sentence signal the hypothetical. If you are unsure about which forms to use, consult the guide to forming conditional verb phrases in this unit.

PROBLEM 4. A conditional form has not been used in a later sentence to show an additional result of a condition that appeared in an earlier sentence.

Incorrect: If our instructor gave us a test today (condition), she would find that we have not yet mastered the conditional (result). We <u>will</u> probably all <u>fail</u>.

Correct: If our instructor gave us a test today, she would find that we have not yet mastered the conditional. We <u>would</u> probably all <u>fail</u>. (The conditional form must be used in the second sentence because it, too, is a result based on the condition in the preceding sentence. That is, *We would probably all fail <u>if our instructor gave us a test today</u>.*)

Self-help Strategy: Make sure that you use a conditional verb phrase in all the result clauses that are based on that particular condition whether or not the *if* clause is repeated.

PROBLEM 5. The verb phrase in the conditional sentence has a verb-form error.

    Incorrect: If Christi <u>had not come</u> to class, she <u>would ne̶ver had known</u> an
                     essay draft was due.

    Correct: If Christi <u>had not come</u> to class, she <u>would never have known</u>
                    an essay draft was due.

    Incorrect: They <u>would have cook</u> dinner for us if we <u>had ask</u> them.

    Correct: They <u>would have cooked</u> dinner for us if we <u>had asked</u> them.

Self-help Strategy: Always check the verb phrase in both clauses to make sure that you not only have chosen the correct verb form for the conditional but that you also have not made any errors in verb form. If you are unsure, consult the *Guide to Forming the Verb Phrase in Conditional Sentences* in this unit.

Understanding the Meaning and Use of Conditional Sentences

A conditional sentence expresses either a real or a hypothetical condition and gives the result of that condition.

The Meaning and Use of Real Conditional Sentences

A real situation by definition exists or has the strong possibility of existing. Real conditional sentences allow the writer to express the following:

general facts or habitual actions

    If my neighbor plays loud rock music, I complain. (habitual action)
    If milk is left out on the counter, it goes sour. (general fact)
    (*When* or *whenever* can be substituted for *if* in these sentences.)

inferences

    If that bird has a red head, it must be a woodpecker.
    If the house was dark, they must have already left for vacation.
    If that book is the correct one, I bought the wrong one.
    (*When* or *whenever* cannot be substituted for *if* in these sentences.)

commands or instructions

    If your laboratory experiment fails, try it again tomorrow.

a future possibility or a prediction

    If my neighbor plays loud music, I will complain.
    If you do not study tonight, you will do poorly on your exam tomorrow.
    If you have not attended class regularly, you may fail the midterm.

The Meaning and Use of Hypothetical Conditional Sentences

A hypothetical situation does not exist or is not likely to exist. Hypothetical conditional sentences allow the writer to achieve the following purposes:

1. **To express what might happen in the present or future as the result of a given condition. In the writer's mind, it is not very likely that the situation will exist or the event will happen.**

   Examples: If my neighbor started to play loud rock music, I would complain to the apartment manager. (I have little reason to believe she will start playing rock music, but this is the action I would take.)

   If instructors taught fewer classes, they could write more comments on their students' papers. (Teachers would no doubt write more comments on papers, but it is highly unlikely that teachers will have the number of classes they teach reduced.)

   Note: In both the example sentences above, the real conditional can be used. However, when using the real conditional, the writer sees the situation as more likely to exist or the event as more likely to happen.

2. **To express an impossible or counterfactual condition and the result of that condition.**

   Examples: If I were you, I would move out of that apartment. (I am not you, but this is what I would do in this situation.)

   If George Washington saw the White House today, he would not recognize it. (George Washington cannot return to life to see the White House today, but since his day, the White House has completely changed.)

   Note: The real conditional cannot be used in the example sentences above because these conditions cannot be made possible or true.

3. **To imagine what could have happened in a past situation but never did.**

   Example: If Sang had not reviewed the conditional before the quiz, he would have lost ten points. (Sang did review it and he did not lose ten points.)

Guide to Forming the Verb Phrase in Conditional Sentences

Forming the Verb or Verb Phrase in Real Conditional Sentences

In real conditional sentences, the sequence of tenses varies according to the meaning of the conditional sentence, as shown on the following page.

1. **To express a general fact or a habitual action**

Condition Clause	Result Clause
same tense	same tense

Examples: If I <u>drink</u> coffee after dinner, I <u>cannot sleep</u>. (fact)
If a caterpillar <u>matures,</u> it <u>becomes</u> a chrysalis. (fact)
Whenever my roommate <u>studied</u> late, I <u>stayed up</u> too. (habitual action)

Note: *When* and *whenever* are often used instead of *if* to express a habitual action.

2. **To make an inference**

Condition Clause	Result Clause
present	must or should + base form
past	must have + past participle

Examples: If it <u>is</u> Tuesday, I must <u>go</u> to my French class.
If that <u>was</u> Mr. Rivera, he <u>must have lost</u> weight.

3. **To give a command or instructions**

Condition Clause	Result Clause
present tense	imperative
past tense	
present perfect	

Examples: If you <u>miss</u> the lecture, <u>go</u> to the teacher's office hours.
If you <u>missed</u> the lecture, <u>go</u> to the teacher's office hours.
If you <u>have missed</u> the lecture, <u>go</u> to the teacher's office hours.

4. **To show a future possibility or make a prediction**

Condition Clause	Result Clause
present	will, can, should, could, may, might + base form
present progressive	
present perfect	

Examples: If I <u>don't study</u> these problems, I <u>will fail</u> my math exam.

If Andreas <u>is telephoning</u> me now, he <u>will get</u> a busy signal.

If you <u>have not finished</u> your term paper by Monday, you <u>will risk</u> getting a lower grade.

Note: A conditional sentence with the modal *will* expresses the strongest possibility. The other modals indicate a lesser degree of possibility.

Examples: If Mina <u>is</u> not <u>attending</u> class regularly, she <u>could fail</u> the course.

If Gerald <u>doesn't do</u> this lab report, he <u>may get</u> a lower grade.

If the letter <u>has</u> not <u>come</u> by now, it <u>might</u> not <u>arrive</u> at all.

Forming the Verb or Verb Phrase in Hypothetical Conditional Sentences

In hypothetical conditional sentences, the time of the sentence is not related to the verb tense used. For example, in the sentence *If I were you* (condition), *I would go* (result), *were* does not signal past time but, instead, a condition that is contrary to fact. The same is true for the sentence *If I had been there* (condition), *she would not have won* (result); in this sentence, *had been* does not signal an event that happened before another in the past but rather is used to speculate about an event that happened in the past.

1. **To express a present or future hypothetical or contrary-to-fact situation**

   Note: In the condition clause, when the simple past form or the past progressive form is used, *were* is used for all forms of *be*.

Condition Clause	Result Clause
simple past form	would, could, might + base form
	would, could, might + be + base form + *ing*
past progressive form	would, could, might + base form
	would, could, might + be + base form + *ing*
could, would + base form	would, could, might + base form

Examples: If I <u>were</u> you, I <u>would study</u> harder for next week's test.

If Tran <u>lived</u> at home instead of in the dormitory, she <u>would have</u> a quiet place to study.

If Abdul <u>started</u> his papers earlier, he <u>would</u> not always <u>be searching</u> for reference materials at the last minute.

If Sheila <u>were</u> not <u>working</u> in the dining hall, she <u>could</u> not <u>afford</u> college.

If Ara <u>were living</u> in the dormitory instead of at home, he <u>would</u> not <u>be spending</u> so much time driving.

If Mike <u>could find</u> his library card, he <u>would start</u> his term paper.

2. **To express a hypothetical situation in the past**

Note: Even though the past perfect tense is used in the *if* clause, it does not show that one event took place before another in the past. It is used to signal that the writer is making a hypothesis or speculation about what would have resulted if a past event had happened differently.

Condition Clause	Result Clause
past perfect form	would, could, might + have + past participle
	would, could, might + have + been + base form + *ing*
past perfect progressive form	could, would, might + have + past participle
	could, would, might + have + been + base form + *ing*

Examples: If Gail <u>had turned</u> her lab report in on time, she <u>would have received</u> the full ten points on it.

If Lan <u>had</u> not <u>refused</u> to loan us his car, we <u>could have been driving</u> to the beach right now.

Natasha <u>might have enjoyed</u> the movie if she <u>had</u> not <u>been concentrating</u> so hard on understanding what the actors were saying.

If Ara <u>had been paying</u> attention in class, he <u>would</u> not <u>have been asking</u> his friends how to do the assignment last night.

Additional Guidelines:

1. Although *if* is the most commonly used conjunction to express the conditional, other conjunctions, such as *even if, when, whenever, whether,* and *unless* (meaning "if . . . not"), also can be used.

Examples: Whether it rains or not, I will still go to the movies.
(I will go [result] regardless of the weather [condition].)
Unless I find my keys, I cannot unlock my bike.
(I must have my keys [condition] to unlock my bike [result].)
(If I do not find my keys, I cannot unlock my bike.)

2. A conditional sentence can be formed without using *if* by reversing the subject and the verb in the *if* clause. This formation is most commonly used with *had* and *should.*

   Examples: Had I known the test was today, I would have studied the chapter.

   Should the telephone ring while I am out, please answer it.

3. It may sometimes be necessary to mix conditional types. The most common mixing involves a past condition and a present result.

   Example: If I had eaten breakfast this morning, my stomach would not be growling. (I did not eat breakfast earlier this morning, so my stomach is growling now.)

■ PART III: Exercises

In Part III, you will practice

- *recognizing and correcting errors with the conditional in individual sentences*
- *completing conditional sentences*
- *producing conditional sentences using given information*
- *recognizing and correcting conditional-sentence errors in a paragraph*

EXERCISE I (Do this exercise on your own. Then check your answers with a classmate.)

Directions: Test your understanding of the meaning and formation of conditional sentences by deciding if each sentence is correct (C) or incorrect (I). Then cross out the errors and correct them.

Example: __I__ If the teacher had not been ill, he would ~~had~~ *have* come to class.

   __C__ Bob would have received a better grade if he had attended class regularly.

_____1. If I have a car, I would not ask friends to take me shopping.

_____2. If Margaret had slept more, she would not have trouble staying awake during the chemistry lecture yesterday.

_____3. When it is hot outside, I drink plenty of water.

_____4. If I will go to Los Angeles next week, I will see all my friends.

_____5. If Peter went to the bookstore later today, he can buy two tapes for the price of one.

_____6. If Edith had not had to turn in her paper today, she would had skipped class.

_____7. If the weather is nice, Marcella always took a walk after dinner.

_____8. If I could found a ride home this weekend, I would give my parents a surprise visit.

_____9. If the teacher had not stopped us right at ten o'clock, I would have been able to finish the test.

_____10. If I were going to a junior college, I would be living at my parents' home.

EXERCISE 2 (Do this exercise on your own. Then check your answers with a classmate.)

Directions: Complete each conditional sentence below by giving the correct form of the verb indicated in parentheses. If you are having problems, review what you learned in *Part II*.

Example: If the weather is nice tomorrow, we __*will hold*__ (hold) class outside.

---

1. If the city _____ (expand) the parking space downtown, we would not have had to park so far away from the movies.

2. When my roommate _____ (snore) loudly, I cannot sleep.

3. Celebrities often get very depressed if they _____ not _____ (appear) in the news.

4. If we _____ not _____ (have) to take an exam on the conditional, we might not have learned it.

5. Maya _____ not _____ (pass) her driving test unless she calms down.

6. If it _____ (be) winter, all these trees would be covered with snow.

7. Had it not rained, the farmers _____ (lose) all their crops.

8. If the airplane had not had a mechanical problem, we _____ probably _____ (arrive) in Tucson by now.

9. We _____ (lie) on the beach in Mexico right now if we had been able to get our visas on time.

10. I _____ (try) to find more opportunities to speak English if I were you.

EXERCISE 3 (Do this exercise with a classmate.)

Directions: Practice your understanding of the formation and meaning of conditional sentences by completing the following sentences.

> **Example:** If I were the instructor of this class, *I would let the students out early today.*

1. If Jennifer did not have to be in class right now, _____

_____

2. I would have gotten to class earlier if _____

_____

3. If I had gotten enough sleep last night, _____

_____

4. I would complain about this class if _____

_____

5. If Vincent has time later, _____

_____

6. If I had had time during the weekend, _____

_____

7. If I had a little extra money, _____

_____

8. If students are given too much to learn, _____

_____

9. If the tuition were raised, _____

_____

10. Even if the professor had canceled class on Tuesday, _____

_____

EXERCISE 4 (Do this exercise on your own. Then check your answers with a classmate.)

Directions: Test your ability to construct a conditional sentence based on information you have been given. In each exercise, you are given a situation and a question. Think through the problem and construct appropriate conditional sentences; in some cases, you can use either a real conditional sentence or a hypothetical conditional sentence.

Example

Problem: Carmen would like to go to the movies tonight, but she has a test in calculus tomorrow.

Question: Should Carmen go to the movies tonight?

Conditional sentences that examine the problem:

If Carmen goes to the movies tonight, she might do poorly on her calculus test tomorrow. (real conditional sentence)

If Carmen went to the movies tonight, she would relax and could do very well on her calculus test tomorrow. (hypothetical conditional sentence)

Exercise 4, continued

1. Problem: The weather forecaster has just announced that it might rain tomorrow. George and Anita have planned a picnic.

   Question: Should George and Anita plan to go on their picnic tomorrow?

   Conditional Sentences: _____

   _____

   _____

2. Problem: Martin is driving on the freeway. The next exit is the one he wants, but he is in the middle lane and the traffic is heavy.

   Question: Should Martin try to exit now?

   Conditional Sentences: _____

   _____

   _____

3. Problem: Mark bought a computer last year and put himself in debt for $2,000. Now he has doubts about having bought the computer.

   Question: Did Mark make the right decision?

   Conditional Sentences: _____

   _____

   _____

4. Problem: Chi Wai lives in an apartment. All his friends live in the dormitory, and now he is lonely.

   Question: Should Chi Wai move to the dormitory?

   Conditional Sentences: _____

   _____

   _____

EXERCISE 5 (Do this exercise with a classmate.)

Directions: The following paragraph, adapted from a student's essay about what students should consider when they choose a major, contains errors in the use of the conditional. Test your knowledge of the meaning and formation of the conditional by circling and correcting these errors.

Another point students should consider when they choose a major is not whether it will make them rich but whether it will at least ensure them enough income to support themselves and their family. It is true that liberal arts majors often get lower-paying jobs than do science majors; however, if people were interested in the liberal arts, they should study those majors. Even though the jobs they get might not enable them to buy big houses or fancy cars, the jobs would allow them to support themselves easily. For instance, my cousin who majored in English now writes novels and is going to publish his first novel in July. Although he has gone through many hardships as a writer, he still has enough income to support his family. He likes writing very much and wants to write as long as he lives. Even though his parents wanted him to become a doctor, it would have been hard for my cousin if he majored in biology. He would probably be very uncomfortable and feel pressured and stressed in his classes. If he then get a job he did not like in that field, he might earn a high salary but he might have found himself with an ulcer. If we looked at my cousin as an example, it becomes clear that students must choose a major that is mentally satisfying, not a major that guarantees a big income.

Exercise 5, continued

Practice with Conditional Sentences

Answer each question with a short written response. Check your conditional sentences carefully for formation of the conditional and then share them with a classmate.

1. If a student has chosen a major to please others, what could be some possible results of that decision?
2. If a student chooses a major that he or she likes, what are usually the results of that decision?

■ PART IV: Writing Activity

In Part IV, you will

- *plan and write a response to a selected topic*
- *share your writing with a classmate*
- *edit your writing for content and sentence-level accuracy*

Step 1—Choosing a Writing Topic

Select one or more of the following:

Topic A: If you had the power to change anything in your country or in the United States, what would you most like to change and why? (Alternatively, you could choose to change something in your school or workplace.)

Topic B: Using what you have learned from your reading or from watching television programs, answer the following question: If we humans do not conserve our natural resources, what will some of the effects be?

Topic C: People often like to speculate about what would have happened if something else had not happened. Think about a significant event in the world, in your own country of origin, in the United States, or in your own life, and imagine what would have happened had this event not occurred.

Topic D: If you have a problem, with whom do you usually share your problem and why?

Topic E: If you could travel anywhere in the world, where would you go and why?

Step 2—Gathering Information

Once you have selected a topic, discuss it with a classmate or in a small group. For Topic A, for example, discuss what you would most like to change, in which country, and why. Be sure to explain your choice carefully to your classmate or your group.

Step 3—Prewriting

Working by yourself, list two or three three reasons why you would make the change you have chosen. Under each reason, jot down examples that illustrate your point.

Step 4—Writing Your First Draft

Using your list of reasons and examples from prewriting, write your first draft. Focus on content.

Step 5—Sharing Your Draft

Working with a classmate, read each other's draft. Give feedback to each other by completing the following:

   A. Reading for Content
1. What did you like most about this draft?
2. What would you still like to know more about?
3. What suggestions do you have for the writer?

   B. Checking for Errors in Conditional Sentences
1. Circle any errors in conditional sentences.
2. Discuss how to correct them.

Step 6—Revising Your Writing

Using your classmate's suggestions as well as your own ideas for revising, write your second draft. Focus on content and sentence-level accuracy. Be especially careful to check any conditional sentences that you have used and to correct errors that you find in them.

Step 7—Proofreading Your Final Draft

Read your final draft once again, looking in particular at conditional sentences. Make any necessary changes.

Postwriting Activity

Step 1—When your paper is returned, check to see if your instructor has marked any errors in conditional sentences.

Step 2—If so, review the material in *Part II* of this unit.

Step 3—Correct each error with the conditional by rewriting the sentence that contains the error. If you are unsure of the correction, ask your instructor for help.

■ PART V: Applying What You Have Learned to Other Writing Assignments

In Part V, you will

- look for and correct errors with conditional sentences in other writing assignments you have done

If you are in a composition class or another class in which you do writing, take your last paper and follow these directions:

1. Check whether your instructor has marked any errors in conditional sentences on your paper. If so, try to correct them, using the material you have learned in this chapter as a guide.

2. If your instructor has not marked any errors in conditional sentences, reread the paper and find any clauses that begin with *if*. Try to determine whether the conditional sentence is formed correctly. If you are not sure, ask a classmate or your instructor.

3. When you do writing assignments in the future, be sure to check **both** clauses of your conditional sentences to make sure that you have formed the verb phrases correctly.

UNIT 5: SENTENCE STRUCTURE*

*ss = grading symbol for sentence-structure errors

■ PART I: What You Need to Know About Errors in Sentence Structure

> ### In Part I, you will answer the following questions:
> - What is a sentence-structure error?
> - Why is it important to avoid sentence-structure errors in writing?
> - What are some strategies for mastering sentence structure?

Definition of the Error

A sentence-structure error (**ss**) is an error in which some aspect of the grammatical structure of a sentence is incorrect. Some examples of errors in sentence structure are missing sentence parts, problems in the formation of relative or noun clauses, unnecessary repetition of the subject of a sentence, an incorrect structure after a given verb, or problems with parallel structure.

You need to be aware that sentences marked sentence structure may also have other errors, but your instructor may choose not to mark them. For instance, an overall problem with sentence structure occurs in the sentence *There is questions concerning the possible dangers of this machines may bring*, in that a relative clause is needed after *dangers* (*dangers that these machines may bring*). In addition, the sentence contains a subject-verb agreement error (*there is questions*), a number error (*this machines*), and a word-choice error (*bring*). The most serious of these problems is the incorrect sentence structure.

Importance of Mastering Sentence Structure in Writing

Sentence-structure errors are global (more serious) errors. As such, they not only cause readers great difficulty in understanding a piece of writing but also are highly noticeable to readers. In the sentence *The thought of my writing will put smiles on people's faces motivates me to write well*, the reader has to go back and replace *of my writing* with *that my writing* to comprehend the sentence. Thus the reader must edit the text while reading its content. Sentence-structure errors are also highly noticeable to readers of formal written English because they expect writers in the academic and professional worlds to have good control of sentence structure. Thus, ESL writers who are having difficulty with sentence-structure errors will want to give high priority to reducing these errors in their writing.

Suggestions for Mastering Sentence Structure

Try to determine if there is a pattern in the sentence-structure errors you are making. A good strategy is to examine your essays and ask yourself whether your sentence-structure errors are of one particular type or of several different types. If you cannot determine whether your errors are similar to any of the types covered in this unit, you will need to ask your instructor or a tutor to help you discover the kind(s) of sentence-structure errors you are making.

Once you know what your sentence-structure problems are, you can study specific rules in this unit. If you need a more detailed analysis of a particular point than this unit provides, you can look up that particular point in an advanced ESL grammar book.

You can also better understand the errors you are making by trying to figure out why you are making them. For example, perhaps you are having difficulty with leaving out or repeating the subject of a sentence because such a structure is permitted in your native language. Another strategy that is very effective, although you may not notice its impact on your writing immediately, is reading extensively in English. Reading will help you become more familiar with English sentence structure and improve your ability to use it correctly in your own writing.

**TEST YOUR UNDERSTANDING
OF SENTENCE–STRUCTURE ERRORS**

After you have read *Part I*, write answers to the following questions. Share your answers with another student.

1. What is a sentence-structure error? Explain in your own words.
2. What are some types of sentence-structure errors that ESL writers may make?
3. Why should ESL writers pay particular attention to sentence-structure errors?
4. Do you think you make sentence-structure errors when you write? If so, what kind do you make?
5. How can you improve your command of English sentence structure?

■ PART II: Common Problems, Rules, and Self-help Strategies

> ### In Part II, you will
> * study eight problems ESL writers commonly have with sentence structure
> * learn selected rules and self-help strategies for controlling sentence structure in writing

This section presents eight problems that ESL writers commonly have with sentence structure. First, study each problem and the examples that illustrate it. Then mark the problems you think you have when you write in English. Remember that if you become aware of the type of sentence-structure errors you most often make, you will increase your chances of avoiding these errors in your writing.

PROBLEM 1.   The verb *to be* is missing.

Incorrect: [My cousin probably a very rich man] since he owned many homes and drove a Mercedes.

Correct: My cousin <u>was</u> probably a very rich man since he owned many homes and drove a Mercedes.

Incorrect: [There many majors] to choose from on this campus.

Correct: There <u>are</u> many majors to choose from on this campus.

Self-help Strategy: If the verb *to be* does not exist in your native language, you will want to be particularly careful not to omit it when it is needed in English.

PROBLEM 2.   The subject of a sentence or clause is missing.

Incorrect: [When we meet new people and start living in a totally new environment are scary.]

Correct: <u>Meeting</u> new people and <u>living</u> in a totally new environment are scary.

Note: In the incorrect sentence above, the adverb clause beginning with *when* cannot be the subject of the verb *are*. Thus, the sentence does not have a subject.

Incorrect: [When realized his son was frequently skipping class,] Mr. Simon was angry.

Correct: [When <u>he</u> realized his son was frequently skipping class,] Mr. Simon was angry.

Incorrect: [Is an interesting class.]⁽ˢˢ⁾ I am learning a great deal.

Correct: <u>It</u> is an interesting class. I am learning a great deal.

Self-help Strategy: A verb always needs a subject when you are making a statement in English. The verb *to be* sometimes requires the "dummy subject" *it* as in the example above or in the structure [*it is* + adjective] (*It is easy* to park on campus. *It is useful* to have a dictionary.)

PROBLEM 3. The subject of a sentence has been unnecessarily repeated.

Incorrect: [<u>My roommate</u> when <u>he</u> is not busy]⁽ˢˢ⁾ with his school work, he is working a part-time job.

Correct: When my roommate is not busy with his school work, he is working a part-time job.

Self-help Strategy: In conversation, English speakers sometimes do repeat the subject of a sentence as in the incorrect example above. In formal writing, however, this kind of repetition is incorrect.

PROBLEM 4. Words in a sentence are missing.

Note: Missing subjects are covered in Problem 2.

Incorrect: They don't want their children to grow up [in a broken family⁽ˢˢ⁾ father's or mother's love.]

Correct: They don't want their children to grow up in a broken family <u>without</u> a father's or mother's love.

Incorrect: He also knew that he didn't possess [enough power to against⁽ˢˢ⁾ the current government.]

Correct: He also knew that he didn't possess enough power to <u>fight</u> against the current government.

PROBLEM 5. A relative clause (also called an adjective clause) is missing or incorrectly formed.

Note: Your instructor may mark this error **ss (rel clause)**.

a. A relative clause is missing.

Incorrect: Alienation is also noticeable among [people come from different cultural backgrounds.]⁽ˢˢ ⁽ʳᵉˡ ᶜˡᵃᵘˢᵉ⁾⁾

Correct: Alienation is also noticeable among people <u>who</u> come from different cultural backgrounds.

Incorrect: *ss (rel clause)*
[There are more than one in three marriages will end in divorce.]

Correct: There are more than one in three marriages <u>that</u> will end in divorce.

Correct: More than one in three marriages will end in divorce. (No relative clause is needed here.)

b. The formation of a relative clause is incorrect.

Incorrect: *ss (rel clause)*
[Cases are found that even good students resort to cheating] in college due to competition and the pressure to get good grades.

Correct: Cases are found <u>in which</u> even good students resort to cheating in college due to competition and the pressure to get good grades.

Incorrect: Whenever I get into [a situation *ss (rel clause)* which is hard to make a decision,] I try to look at it from different perspectives.

Correct: Whenever I get into a situation <u>in which it is</u> hard to make a decision, I try to look at it from different perspectives.

Incorrect: *ss (rel clause)*
I just met [the people who their house] I am planning to rent for the summer.

Correct: I just met the people <u>whose house</u> I am planning to rent for the summer.

c. A noun or a pronoun has been unnecessarily repeated in a relative clause.

Incorrect: *ss (rel clause)*
[The people whom I have met them in my class] are very friendly.

Correct: The people whom I have met in my class are very friendly.

Self-help Strategy: The following rules will give you a brief review of the form and function of relative clauses. Most ESL grammar and writing texts cover relative clause formation fully. You can study relative clauses in one of these texts if you need more information than this text provides on forming relative clauses.

Rules for Relative Clauses

Relative clauses are adjective clauses formed with the relative pronouns *who*, *whom*, *whose*, *which*, or *that* or with the relative adverbs *when*, *where*, or *why*. To use relative pronouns correctly, you need to be aware of their different functions in a relative clause.

1. *Who, that,* and *which* can function as the subject of a relative clause. *Who* refers to people, *that* refers to people and things, and *which* refers only to things.

Examples: The teacher called out the names of those students <u>who</u> [or *that*] were absent. (*Who* [or *that*] refers to students and is the subject of the relative clause.)

The book <u>that</u> (or <u>which</u>) was left on the table is no longer there. (*That* [or *which*] refers to the book and is the subject of the relative clause.)

2. ***Whom, that,* and *which* can function as a direct object in a relative clause. *Whom* refers to people, *that* refers to people and things, and *which* refers only to things.**

Examples: The student <u>whom</u> (or <u>that</u>) they have chosen to be editor of the class newspaper does not want the job. (*Whom* [or *that*] refers to the student and is the direct object of *chosen* in the relative clause. In spoken English, *who* can be used, but should not be used in formal, written English.)

I think the gift <u>that</u> (or <u>which</u>) I found will please Samuel. (*That* [or *which*] is the object of *found* and refers to the gift.)

Notes: *Whom, that,* and *which* may be omitted when they function as direct objects if the writer wishes to do so.

In the relative clauses in Rules 1 and 2 above, *that* is preferable to *which* in current American English.

3. ***Whom* and *which* can function as the object of a preposition in a relative clause. *Whom* refers to persons and *which* refers to things.**

Examples: The person for <u>whom</u> these plane reservations were made never picked up the tickets. (*Whom* is the object of the preposition *for* and refers to the person.)

The history class in <u>which</u> Adela enrolled requires a term paper. (*Which* is the object of the preposition *in* and refers to the history class.)

4. ***Whose* functions as a possessive pronoun in a relative clause and refers to people or things.**

Examples: The person <u>whose</u> books are on the table will be back soon. (*Whose* shows that the books belong to the person.)

Eric fixed my car as well as the car <u>whose</u> transmission was broken. (*Whose* shows that the transmission belongs to the car.)

5. **Relative clauses can also be connected to the nouns they modify with the relative adverbs *when, where,* and *why*.**

Examples: The restaurant <u>where</u> we ate is only open for dinner.

Tell me the reason <u>why</u> you had so much difficulty with the exam.

I will never forget the time <u>when</u> the teacher got mad at us in class.

In the example sentences given so far in this section, the information the relative clause added to the sentence is essential, meaning that it is necessary to identify the noun or to distinguish the noun from others of the same type. However, if the relative clause adds additional or extra information to the sentence, it is set off by commas. The first is called a **restrictive** relative clause and the second a **nonrestrictive** relative clause. The sentences below contain nonrestrictive relative clauses. In nonrestrictive relative clauses, *that* is not interchangeable with *who*, *whom*, or *which*.

Examples: My mother, <u>who</u> is ninety-one years old, lives in a retirement community.

The University of California, <u>which</u> is a public school, has nine campuses.

My math professor, <u>who</u> loves to cook, invited us all to dinner at his house.

Thomas Jefferson, <u>whose</u> home was in Virginia, always loved to return there.

Pepe's restaurant, <u>where</u> we often eat, has an excellent buffet.

PROBLEM 6. An incorrect grammatical structure has been used after a verb.

Incorrect: Their acquaintances [assume them as passive, unsociable, and boring.]

Correct: Their acquaintances assume <u>that they are</u> passive, unsociable, and boring.

Correct: Their acquaintances assume <u>them to be</u> passive, unsociable, and boring.

Correct: Their acquaintances <u>see them as</u> passive, unsociable, and boring.

Incorrect: [The author describes that workaholics are] intense, energetic, competitive, and driven.

Correct: The author <u>describes workaholics as</u> intense, energetic, competitive, and driven.

Correct: The author <u>says that workaholics are</u> intense, energetic, competitive, and driven.

^{ss}

Incorrect: [He worried about that his classmates would start] to dislike him.

Correct: He worried <u>that</u> his classmates <u>would start</u> to dislike him.

Correct: He worried <u>about</u> his classmates <u>starting</u> to dislike him.

Self-help Strategy: Certain verbs need to be followed by a specific structure (or choice of structures), such as a noun clause or an object plus an infinitive phrase. As you can see in the example sentences above, the structure is often dictated by the verb itself. For example, the verb *assume* in the first example above can be followed by either a noun clause or an object plus an infinitive phrase.

Many common verbs are followed by noun clauses. A noun clause begins with the word *that* and functions as a subject or an object.

Examples: (noun clauses are underlined):

<u>That you have graduated</u> makes the whole family proud.

We concluded <u>that the experimental design was flawed</u>.

The following common verbs are often followed by noun clauses:

assume We assume <u>that you will graduate next June</u>.

believe My professor believes <u>that my research is ready to be published</u>.

conclude As a result of their study, the researchers concluded <u>that the pesticide under study can be harmful to humans</u>.

doubt I doubt <u>that the experiment has been properly designed</u>.

feel Many voters feel <u>that their votes do not truly count</u>.

hope We hope <u>that our research will be published in a major journal</u>.

insist The defense attorney insisted <u>that the evidence should not be allowed in court</u>.

know For a long time, scientists have known <u>that the San Andreas fault could produce a major earthquake</u>.

realize Mr. Matthew's supervisors realize <u>that he is one of their most valuable employees</u>.

say Roger said <u>that he could assist with the field work</u>.

suggest The results of the study suggest <u>that eating broccoli can help prevent cancer</u>.

think The committee members think <u>that a fund-raising drive is necessary</u>.

worry We were worried <u>that you had gotten lost</u>.

PROBLEM 7. Two clauses have been used that do not fit together grammatically.

> *Note*: This error is sometimes called *mixed sentence structure*.
>
> Incorrect: [As my brother said to my mom that he did not feel like having a family.]
>
> Correct   My brother said to my mom that he did not feel like having a family.
>
> Correct: As my brother said to my mom, he does not feel like having a family.

PROBLEM 8. A structure has been used that is not parallel to other structures in the sentence.

> *Note*: Your instructor may mark their kind of error **ss** (**not //**).
>
> Incorrect: My advisor told me to check out a journal from the library [and that reading it as soon as possible was necessary.]
>
> Correct: My advisor told me <u>to check out</u> a journal from the library and <u>to read</u> it as soon as possible.
>
> Incorrect: Most successful students are skilled at taking notes, summarizing, [and are able to read critically.]
>
> Correct: Most successful students are skilled at <u>taking</u> notes, <u>summarizing</u>, and <u>reading</u> critically.

Guide to Using Parallel Structure

Whenever one or more items in a sentence are joined by the words *and*, *but*, *or*, *nor*, *yet*, these parts of the sentence should be parallel in structure. That is, they should have the same grammatical form (for example, all infinitives, all noun clauses, or all prepositional phrases).

Examples of Parallel Structure

Verbs (infinitives):
 I like <u>to swim</u>, <u>to surf</u>, and <u>to water-ski</u>.

Verbs (base forms):
 I like to <u>swim</u>, <u>surf</u>, and <u>water-ski</u>.

Verbs (gerunds):
 I enjoy <u>swimming</u>, <u>surfing</u>, and <u>waterskiing</u>.

Verbs (present participles):

While he was <u>thinking about</u> the class lectures and reviewing some articles, he got an idea for his term paper.

Prepositional phrases:

Nowadays, computers are used heavily <u>by many people</u> and <u>in many different ways</u>.

Noun clauses:

Professor Allen has promised <u>that the exam will be graded by 5 P.M.</u> and <u>that the scores will be posted outside his office by 5:30 P.M.</u>

Adjectives:

The teacher is <u>friendly</u> and <u>helpful</u>, but somewhat <u>disorganized</u>.

■ PART III: Exercises

> ## In Part III, you will practice
>
> - *recognizing and correcting sentence-structure errors in sentences*
> - *using relative clauses correctly*
> - *using parallel structure*
> - *recognizing and correcting sentence-structure errors in a paragraph*

EXERCISE I (Do this exercise on your own. Then check your answers with a classmate.)

Directions: The following sentences contain sentence-structure errors. First, decide whether a sentence is correct (C) or incorrect (I). Then correct the incorrect sentences by rewriting the complete sentence correctly below the original sentence. (**Note:** The sentences in this exercise cover the different types of sentence-structure errors presented in this unit. For exercises on relative clauses and parallel structure only, see Exercises 2 and 3.)

  __I__ 1. Molecular genetics is a field is progressing very fast.

     Molecular genetics is a field that (OR which) is progressing very fast.

_____2. To know their native language should be proud instead of embarrassed.

_____

_____

_____3. Whenever I see the colors red and green, which always remind me of Christmas.

_____

_____

_____4. Most children I know who grew up in strict families have become successful.

_____

_____

_____5. She wonders whether studying so hard worth it.

_____

_____

_____6. Wong is a Chinese woman who grew up in the United States finds her native language very difficult.

_____

_____

_____7. Engineering 10 is the course that I spend the least time on it.

_____

_____

_____8. Room 194 Chemistry is one of the largest classrooms on my campus, that can hold around 500 students.

_____

_____

_____9. There are two reasons for scary of writing English.

_____

_____

_____10. To go to school and working full time is hard.

_____

_____

_____11. As grow up, many children develop attitudes they will later have as adults.

_____

_____

_____12. Laura, an illiterate single parent, is unable to read the letters she receives from the hospital telling her that her oldest son needs medical treatment.

_____

_____

_____13. To improve her reading skills, Laura could enroll in a night-school literacy class or look for a volunteer who could tutor her at home.

_____

_____

_____14. The engineering professor assumes in the students have a strong background in mathematics.

_____

_____

_____15. Space-shuttle astronauts need to be prepared for every obstacle that will encounter.

_____

_____

_____16. A person is impossible to live without being influenced by the society around him or her.

_____

_____

_____17. Many high-school students are more interested in learning about current events than about events happened in the past.

_____

_____

_____18. The editor doubts about the article being of interest to many of the readers of the magazine.

_____

_____

_____19. When she has spare time, Antonia likes to take bike rides, read novels, and visit her friends.

_____

_____

_____20. As we can see that Marcella is very lucky to have gotten a full scholarship for four years of college work.

_____

_____

EXERCISE 2 (Do this exercise with a classmate.)

A. Directions: Read the following sentences, some of which have parallel-structure problems. Correct any problems in parallel structure by rewriting the incorrect sentences.

1. That Jack arrived late to the meeting and his not being prepared angered his supervisor.

_____

_____

2. I hope to introduce you to Dr. Wood, my thesis advisor and who chairs the Chemistry Department.

_____

_____

3. In college, what classes you take and when you take them is generally your own decision.

_____

_____

4. His summer job involves washing laboratory equipment, to set up new experiments, and recording some basic data.

_____

_____

5. Growing up in a large family and working parents resulted in Elizabeth's not getting much individual attention from her parents.

_____

_____

B. Directions: Complete the following sentences in your own words. Make sure you use parallel structure.

1. Three things I enjoy doing on weekends are _____

_____

2. Two things I have learned since I have been a student here are_____

_____

3. In my opinion, a good teacher must be _____

_____

EXERCISE 3 (Do this exercise on your own. Then check your answers with a classmate.)

A. Directions: Fill in the blanks with the correct relative pronoun *(who, whom, whose, which, that)*. In some cases, more than one answer is possible.

1. Mark thanked the tutor _____ had worked with him an hour per week for the whole semester.

2. Dr. Ruiz is the professor _____ economics course I am planning to take next semester.

3. The person with _____ I share a locker is over there.

4. The backpack _____ is on the chair is mine.

5. Portland is a city _____ residents tend to be environmentally aware.

B. Directions: Combine each of the following sets of sentences into one sentence using a relative clause.

Example: The Sherpa guide stayed behind with the hikers. The hikers were too tired to hike any farther.
The Sherpa guide stayed behind with the hikers who were too tired to hike any farther. OR *The Sherpa guide stayed behind with the hikers, who were too tired to hike any farther.*

---

1. Genetic engineering is a newly developed technology. It is expected to help immensely in agriculture.

   _____

   _____

2. The man is a lawyer. I am renting his house.

   _____

3. The people were late. We were waiting for them.

   _____

4. She borrowed a bicycle. Its tires were slightly flat.

   _____

5. Today, Michael plans to do the lab experiment. He was unable to do the experiment last week.

   _____

   _____

6. The student was asked to make a speech at commencement. The student got the highest grades in the class.

   _____

   _____

7. Some bike riders do not stop at stop signs. These bike riders may be given either a warning or a ticket.

   _____

   _____

C. **Directions:** Identify any problems with relative clauses in the following sentences. If a sentence is correct, write C. If it is incorrect, rewrite the sentence correctly.

1. The person whom I went to the movies fell asleep during the film.

   _____

   _____

2. A student who plagiarizes on a paper will fail the paper and possibly the whole course which he wrote the paper.

   _____

   _____

3. The man whom I met last night and who immigrated to the United States a year ago speaks English well.

   _____

   _____

4. I wrote a thank-you note to the people whom I visited their home over the Christmas holidays.

   _____

   _____

5. The instructor teaches that course is very well organized.

   _____

   _____

EXERCISE 4 (Do this exercise on your own. Then check your answers with a classmate.)

Directions: The following paragraph, written by a student, has been edited so that the only errors are in sentence structure. First, find the eight sentence-structure errors in the paragraph, and mark a star at the beginning of each incorrect sentence. Then rewrite each incorrect sentence below the paragraph. The first one has been done for you.

*Some couples are childless have made a decision not to have children. This kind of family rapidly growing in the United States. These couples choose to be childless for various reasons. However, I personally have a hard time understanding people choose to live without children.

Many couples think that this world is not "good enough" for children to grow up in. Other couples think that too much time and money to raise children. Still others want to focus on developing their careers rather than raise children.

I find it hard to understand these reasons that not having children. For me, having children one of the most essential parts of life. It would be hard for me to view a career as being more important than having a family of my own. I am sure I would feel disappointed with my life when I got old if I did not have children or grandchildren. I understand that the world overpopulation, but having children is one of our basic instincts. Although I do not want many children, I certainly hope to have one or two of my own.

Revised sentences:

1. *Some couples who (OR that) are childless have made a decision not to have children.*

2. _____

   _____

3. _____

   _____

4. _____

   _____

5. _____

_____

6. _____

_____

7. _____

_____

8. _____

_____

■ PART IV: Writing Activity

In Part IV, you will
- *plan and write a response to a selected topic*
- *share your writing with a classmate*
- *edit your writing for content and sentence-level accuracy*

Step 1—Choosing a Writing Topic

Select one or more of the following:

Topic A: Write about a current news event. First, summarize the news item. Then explain why it is of interest to you or why it is of particular importance.

Topic B: Most people would agree that we not only learn in formal classroom situations but that much of our learning also goes on outside of school. Write about an important learning experience that you have had outside of the classroom. Explain the experience and what you learned from it.

Topic C: The issue of whether or not students should be required to study a foreign language in school has been controversial in the United States for some time. In fact, in recent years, foreign-language requirements have been dropped at some U.S. schools. Do you think students should be required to take a foreign language in school as a general education requirement? Give reasons to support your point of view.

Step 2—Gathering Information

Once you have selected a topic, discuss it with a classmate or in a small group. For Topic A, discuss the news item you have chosen. Explain why it is of importance or of particular interest to you. For Topic B, discuss an important learning experience that you have had. Explain exactly what you learned from it. For Topic C, discuss whether or not you think students should be required to take a foreign language. Discuss some of the pros and cons of this issue.

Step 3—Prewriting

Working by yourself, list some of the ideas you have discussed with a classmate or in a small group. If you are doing Topic A, make notes on the news item, giving reasons why it is important or of interest to you. If you have chosen Topic B, make notes on the learning experience and what you learned from it. If you are doing Topic C, list the reasons for and against students' studying a foreign language as part of their general education. Then decide what your point of view is and why. If you already know your point of view, write it down and list your reasons for it.

Step 4—Writing Your First Draft

Use your list from prewriting to help you write your first draft. Focus on content.

Step 5—Sharing Your Draft

Working with a classmate, read each other's draft. Give feedback to each other using the format given below.

A. Reading for Content
1. What do you like most about this paper?
2. What would you still like to know more about?
3. What suggestions do you have for the writer?

B. Checking for Errors in Sentence Structure
1. Put brackets [ ] around any sentences that contain sentence-structure errors in your classmate's draft.
2. Discuss how to correct them.

Step 6—Revising Your Writing

Using your classmate's suggestions as well as your own ideas for revising, write your second draft. Focus on content and sentence-level accuracy. As you examine each sentence, be especially aware of any errors in sentence sructure.

Step 7—Proofreading Your Final Draft

Read your final draft once again, paying particular attention to sentence structure. Make any necessary changes.

Postwriting Activity

Step 1—When your paper is returned, check to see if your instructor has marked any errors in sentence structure.

Step 2—If so, review the material in *Part II* of this unit.

Step 3—Correct each sentence-structure error by rewriting the sentence that contains the error. If you are unsure of the correction, ask a classmate or your instructor for help.

■ PART V: Applying What You Have Learned to Other Writing Assignments

In Part V, you will

- look for and correct sentence-structure errors in any other writing assignments you have done

If you are in a composition class or another class in which you do writing, take your last returned paper and follow these directions:

1. Check whether your instructor has marked any sentence-structure errors. If so, try to correct them using the material you have learned in this unit as a guide.

2. If your instructor has not marked any sentence-structure errors, take one paragraph and check the structure of each sentence yourself. Try to determine if the sentence structure is correct. If you are not sure, ask a classmate or your instructor to help you.

3. When you do writing assignments in the future, be sure to check for sentence-structure errors.

UNIT 6: WORD ORDER*

*wo = grading symbol for word-order errors

■ PART I: What You Need to Know About Errors in Word Order

In Part I, you will answer the following questions:
- *What is an error in word order?*
- *Why is it important to avoid word-order errors in writing?*
- *What are some strategies for mastering word order?*

Definition of the Error

A word-order error (**wo**) is one in which the order of words in a sentence is incorrect or awkward. For example, in the sentence *The basketball team was exhausted <u>completely</u> after their game*, the word *completely* is in an incorrect position in the sentence; it should come before the adjective *exhausted*. In the sentence *Mary went <u>yesterday</u> to the library*, the word *yesterday* is in an awkward position in the sentence; it usually comes at the beginning or the end of the sentence.

Importance of Mastering Word Order in Writing

Word-order errors are global (more serious) errors because in some cases they can affect the organization of a whole sentence. For example, in the sentence *Spanish language speak many people in Latin America*, the word order, which is not English word order, affects the whole sentence, making it difficult for the reader to understand. Some word-order errors, however, may not be as serious and may not affect the reader's understanding of the overall sentence. For example, in the sentence *Mary lent to John the book*, the word order is incorrect, but the reader can still easily understand the message. Nevertheless, incorrect or awkward word order, whether serious or less serious, will distract the reader and make a piece of writing difficult to read, particularly if the error is frequent.

Suggestions for Mastering Word Order

Not all ESL writers have serious problems with English word order. Many writers, however, tend to experience problems with word order when using certain grammatical structures, such as indirect questions, adverbs, and adverbial phrases. If you are having problems with word order in these cases, you will find the rules and strategies in *Part II* of this unit helpful.

You may also find it helpful to think about the word order that is used in your native language in order to become aware of any patterns that you might be incorrectly transferring into English from your native language. Keep in mind that in English the basic word order is

Subject + Verb + Object
Gene + is reading + the newspaper.

OR

Subject + Verb + Complement
Gene + is + happy.

In some languages, such as Japanese and Korean, the basic word order is [Subject + Object + Verb]. In other languages, such as Tagalog, the basic word order is [Verb + Subject + Object]. You will also want to keep in mind that even if your native language has the same basic word order as English does, there still may be other differences. For example, Spanish and English have the same basic word order [Subject + Verb + Object]. However, word-order differences still occur. In English, adjectives usually come before the noun they modify as in *These black shoes belong to Jessica,* while in Spanish, adjectives often come after the noun they modify.

If you have numerous problems with word order when you write, perhaps the best way for you to master English word order is by reading extensively. You can focus on the word order used in the writing in your textbooks as well as in other books, magazines, and newspapers.

TEST YOUR UNDERSTANDING OF WORD ORDER

After you have read *Part I*, write answers to the questions below. Share your answers with another student.

1. What is an error in word order? Explain in your own words.
2. How serious are word-order errors?
3. Do you make word-order errors when you write in English?
4. Are there any differences in word order that you know of between English and your native language?
5. What strategies can ESL writers use to reduce word-order errors in their writing?

■ PART II: Common Problems, Rules, and Self-help Strategies

> **In Part II, you will**
>
> ● *study seven problems ESL writers commonly have with word order*
> ● *learn selected rules and self-help strategies for controlling word order in writing*

This section presents seven problems ESL writers commonly have with word order. First, study each problem and the examples that illustrate it. Then mark the problems you think you have when you write in English. Remember that if you become aware of the type of word-order errors you most often make, you will increase your chances of avoiding these errors in your writing.

PROBLEM 1. The word order is incorrect in an indirect question that makes up a noun clause.

Incorrect: When I came home, I wondered [where were my roommates.]
                                                        wo

Correct: When I came home, I wondered <u>where my roommates were</u>.

Incorrect: I don't know [what did the instructor say] about the next lab assignment.
                                          wo

Correct: I don't know <u>what the instructor said</u> about the next lab assignment.

Incorrect: The article does not clearly explain [how was the experiment performed.]
                                                              wo

Correct: The article does not clearly explain <u>how the experiment was performed</u>.

Rule for Word Order in Indirect Questions

An indirect question is sometimes part of a sentence. Always use statement word order (not direct-question word order) for indirect questions. In other words, do not invert the subject and the verb as you would when asking a direct question.

Direct-question word order: Invert the subject and first auxiliary verb.

Examples: Where <u>have you</u> been living?
 <u>Did Paul</u> pass the midterm?

Indirect-question word order: Do **not** invert the subject and verb.

Examples: I don't know where <u>you live</u>.
 I wonder whether <u>Paul passed</u> the midterm.

Some common phrases that can be followed by noun-clause indirect questions include *I wonder, I don't know, I can't remember, I do not understand.*

PROBLEM 2. The pronoun that accompanies a two-word verb (such as *hand in, pick up, throw out*) has been incorrectly placed.

> *Note:* These verbs are often called phrasal verbs, and the prepositions that go with these verbs are called particles.

Incorrect: I don't like these posters anymore. I have decided to [throw out ^{WO} them.]

Correct: I don't like these posters anymore. I have decided to <u>throw them out.</u>

Incorrect: Any student who misses a quiz cannot [make up it.] ^{WO}

Correct: Any student who misses a quiz cannot <u>make it up</u>.

Guidelines for Noun and Pronoun Object Placement with Two-Word (Phrasal) Verbs

The verb and particle of a two-word (phrasal) verb may be always separated, never separated, or optionally separated. If a phrasal verb can be separated and it has an object pronoun, this pronoun will always be located between the verb and the particle. If the phrasal verb is not separable, the pronoun will come after the verb. An ESL dictionary will indicate whether or not a phrasal verb is separable.

1. **Always separated:** The object or object pronoun comes between the verb and its particle.

   Examples: Martha <u>talked</u> her father <u>into</u> letting her use the car.
    Martha <u>talked</u> him <u>into</u> letting her use the car.

   Examples: Let's try <u>to cheer</u> Bill <u>up</u>.
    Let's try <u>to cheer</u> him <u>up</u>.

2. **Can be separated:** The object comes either after the verb and particle or between the verb and particle. An object pronoun always comes between the verb and its particle.

> Examples: Jake said he wanted <u>to think over</u> the situation.
> Jake said he wanted <u>to think</u> the situation <u>over</u>.
> Jake said he wanted <u>to think</u> it <u>over</u>.
>
> I haven't been able <u>to figure out</u> the problem.
> I haven't been able <u>to figure</u> the problem <u>out</u>.
> I haven't been able <u>to figure</u> it <u>out</u>.

3. **Never separated:** The object or object pronoun comes after the verb and its particle.

> Examples: Katya <u>takes after</u> her mother.
> Katya <u>takes after</u> her.
>
> I will need <u>to check into</u> the matter.
> I will need <u>to check into</u> it.

PROBLEM 3. An adverb that modifies an adjective has been incorrectly placed.

> Incorrect: The mayor had become [aware ^{WO} more] of his position in the town.
> Correct: The mayor had become <u>more aware</u> of his position in the town.
> Incorrect: I felt [exhausted ^{WO} completely] after the all-day hike.
> Correct: I felt <u>completely exhausted</u> after the all-day hike.

Rule: An adverb that modifies an adjective precedes the adjective.

> Examples: San Francisco is <u>extremely</u> beautiful.
> This classroom is <u>unusually</u> small.
> They have a <u>completely</u> remodeled kitchen.

PROBLEM 4. An adjective that modifies a noun has been incorrectly placed.

> Incorrect: The [notebook ^{WO} blue] is Jerry's.
> Correct: The <u>blue notebook</u> is Jerry's.
> Incorrect: The [blue ^{WO} large notebook] is Jerry's.
> Correct: The <u>large blue notebook</u> is Jerry's.

Self-help Strategies:
* Remember that adjectives come **before** the nouns they modify in English.

● Review the following guideline for the order of adjectives when more than one adjective modifies a noun:

(number) + (general comment) + (size) + (shape) + (color) + (material) + NOUN

Examples: several high-strength black steel beams
(a) long rectangular grey metal sheet
numerous flashing multicolored lights
several small white and black dogs

PROBLEM 5. The word order is incorrect after a verb that has both a direct object and an indirect object.

Note: The direct object usually refers to a thing and the indirect object usually refers to a person. The indirect object will be preceded by *to* or *for* if it follows the direct object.

Incorrect: The president of the company [gave to Jenna a ^{WO} special assignment.]

Correct: The president of the company gave <u>a special assignment to Jenna</u>.

Correct: The president of the company gave <u>Jenna a special assignment</u>.

Incorrect: Matt [bought for me a ^{WO} present.]

Correct: Matt bought <u>a present for me</u>.

Correct: Matt bought <u>me a present</u>.

Rules for Word Order of Direct and Indirect Objects

Not many verbs in English take both a direct and an indirect object. However, the following two rules will help you master word order in sentences containing both objects.

1. When a verb (V) has both a direct object (DO) and an indirect object (IO), the direct object must come first if the indirect object is preceded by *to* or *for*. If, however, the *to* or *for* is omitted, then the indirect object must come first.

Examples:

The clerk <u>sold</u> <u>a book</u> <u>to me</u>.
(V, DO, IO)

The clerk <u>sold</u> <u>me</u> <u>a book</u>.
(V, IO, DO)

Matt <u>bought</u> <u>a present</u> <u>for me</u>.
(V, DO, IO)

Matt <u>bought</u> <u>me</u> <u>a present</u>.
(V, IO, DO)

Some common verbs that take an indirect object with *to* are *give, write, show, teach, sell, send, lend, bring, hand.*

Some common verbs that take an indirect object with *for* are *buy, get, make, bake.*

2. A small number of verbs must have the indirect object follow the direct object, and this indirect object must be preceded by *to* or *for*. Verbs in this group that take indirect objects with *for* include *answer, open, close.* Verbs in this group that take indirect objects with *to* include *announce, introduce, suggest, mention, describe.*

Incorrect: Richard [explained Mary the math problem.]
Correct: Richard explained <u>the math problem to Mary</u>.
Incorrect: Richard [answered Mary the question.]
Correct: Richard answered <u>the question for Mary</u>.

PROBLEM 6. An adverb has been incorrectly placed.

Incorrect: I went [yesterday] to the movies with Johan.
Correct: I went to the movies with Johan <u>yesterday.</u>
Correct: <u>Yesterday</u> I went to the movies with Johan.
Correct: I went to the movies <u>yesterday</u> with Johan.

Incorrect: [Poorly,] Bill did that cleaning job.
Correct: Bill did that cleaning job <u>poorly.</u>

Guidelines for Placement of Adverbs

Generally, adverbs can be placed in several different positions in a sentence.

Initial position (at the beginning of the sentence)
    Example: <u>Yesterday</u> I sailed for four hours.

Midposition (before the verb or in the middle of the verb phrase)
    Examples: I <u>especially</u> like Boston.
                 I do not <u>really</u> like peanut butter ice cream.

End position (at the end of the sentence)
    Example: I expect my friend to arrive <u>tomorrow.</u>

However, not all adverbs can be placed in all three positions. What follows are some general guidelines for adverb placement according to the function of the adverb.

1. **Adverbs of place** usually take the end position.
   Correct: John is sitting <u>outside</u>.
   Incorrect: <u>Outside</u>^{WO} John is sitting.

   (Other common adverbs of place include *inside, here, there*.)

2. **Adverbs of definite time** usually take the beginning or end position.
   Correct: I went to my aerobics class <u>yesterday</u>.
   Correct: <u>Yesterday</u> I went to my aerobics class.
   Incorrect: I went <u>yesterday</u> to my aerobics class.

   (Other common adverbs of definite time include *today, tomorrow, now*.)

3. **Adverbs of indefinite time** can take the initial, middle, or end position.
   Correct: <u>Recently</u> I've become interested in karate.
   Correct: I've <u>recently</u> become interested in karate.
   Correct: I've become interested in karate <u>recently</u>.

   (Other adverbs of indefinite time include *lately*.)

4. **Adverbs used to evaluate** usually take the end position.
   Correct: Bill did that cleaning job <u>well</u>.
   Incorrect: Bill did <u>well</u> that cleaning job.

   (Other common adverbs used to evaluate include *badly, poorly*.)

5. **Adverbs of Manner** usually take the middle or end position but can take the initial position.
   Correct: Luis <u>quietly</u> opened the door to the baby's room.
   Correct: Luis opened the door to the baby's room <u>quietly</u>.
   Correct: <u>Quietly</u>, Luis opened the door to the baby's room.

   (Other common adverbs of manner include *quickly, carelessly, softly*.)

6. **Adverbs of frequency** follow very specific rules regarding their position in the sentence.
   (Common adverbs of frequency include *always, frequently, occasionally, seldom, continually, hardly ever, often, sometimes, ever, never, rarely, usually*.)
   a. with the verb *to be*—usually after the verb
   Correct: John is <u>never</u> at home when I call him.
   Correct: Vincent is <u>continually</u> busy.

b. with the verb *to be* + *not*—after *not*

Correct:	Brian is not <u>always</u> nice to his little sister.
Correct:	It is not <u>usually</u> so hot here during the summer.

c. with other verbs—before the verb

Correct:	Lois <u>always</u> skates on the boardwalk.
Correct:	I <u>never</u> ride my bicycle to class.

d. in a verb phrase—after the first auxiliary verb

Correct:	Tim is <u>always</u> running out of money when we go out to eat.
Correct:	I have <u>never</u> seen a comet.

e. in a verb phrase with *not*—after *not*

Correct:	Maria does not <u>always</u> type her papers.
Correct:	Mark does not <u>usually</u> have time to read the newspaper.

PROBLEM 7. Adverbial phrases or clauses at the end of a sentence are not in the correct order.

Note: More than one adverbial phrase or clause can occur at the end of a sentence in English. Some of these adverbial phrases or clauses can also occur at the beginning of the sentence. However, usually only one adverbial clause or phrase can occur at the beginning of a sentence.

Incorrect:	Mark lifts weights [<u>to keep in shape</u> ^{WO} <u>every morning.</u>]
Correct:	Mark lifts weights <u>every morning</u> <u>to keep in shape</u>.
Correct:	<u>Every morning</u>, Mark lifts weights <u>to keep in shape</u>.
Correct:	<u>To keep in shape</u>, Mark lifts weights <u>every morning</u>.
Incorrect:	We left the movie [<u>because it was boring</u> ^{WO} <u>before it was over.</u>]
Correct:	We left the movie <u>before it was over</u> <u>because it was boring</u>.
Incorrect:	I walked [<u>this morning</u> ^{WO} <u>to the cafeteria.</u>]
Correct:	I walked <u>to the cafeteria</u> <u>this morning</u>.
Correct:	<u>This morning</u>, I walked <u>to the cafeteria</u>.

Guidelines for Word Order When Several Adverbials Occur at the End of a Sentence

When several adverbials (phrases and/or clauses that function like adverbs) occur at the end of a sentence in English, word-order problems often occur. Although the order of these adverbials in relation to each other sometimes varies, you will find the following guidelines helpful. These guidelines are based on the different types of adverbials listed in the box that follows.

Adverbials of time:	at six o'clock, this morning, in the evening
Adverbials of frequency:	every morning, every Tuesday
Adverbials of position:	in the cafeteria, at home, in the classroom
Adverbials of direction:	to the cafeteria, from the lab
Adverbials of purpose:	(in order) to lose weight, so that I could stay in shape
Adverbials of reason:	because it is hot, because it was interesting

1. Adverbials of time and frequency generally come after adverbials of position and direction.

   Examples: She walks <u>to campus</u> <u>everyday</u> <u>at noon</u>.
   She studies <u>at home</u> <u>every evening</u>.

2. Adverbials of time and frequency are generally interchangeable in terms of position.

   Examples: She walks to campus <u>everyday</u> <u>at noon</u>.
   She walks to campus <u>at noon</u> <u>everyday</u>.

3. Adverbials of purpose and reason generally come after all other adverbials.

   Examples: Mark works out in the gym every night <u>to keep in shape</u>.
   We left the party before 9 P.M. <u>because we had another commitment</u>.

■ PART III: Exercises

> ### In Part III, you will practice
> * *recognizing and correcting word-order errors in sentences*
> * *writing sentences that contain indirect questions*
> * *recognizing and correcting word-order errors in a paragraph*

EXERCISE 1 (Do this exercise on your own. Then check your answers with a classmate.)

Directions: Some of the following sentences have incorrect or awkward word order. If a sentence is incorrect, rewrite the sentence correctly below the original. If a sentence is correct, write *correct* below it.

1. I do not really know what is this issue all about.

    _____

    _____

2. I have been already advanced to candidacy for my Ph.D.

    _____

    _____

3. The only concern I have is how much will it cost the students to pay the rent.

    _____

    _____

4. I ran to the grocery store this morning because I needed some milk for my cereal.

    _____

    _____

5. A potential candidate must consider what his chances for winning the election are.

    _____

    _____

6. Tomas is planning to have for Luis a surprise birthday party.

    _____

    _____

7. I haven't gotten my term paper back even though I handed in it a week ago.

    _____

    _____

8. I am going to buy my father a silk beautiful green tie for his birthday.

    _____

    _____

9. Bill often goes swimming in the evening to get regular exercise.

_____

_____

10. The professor comes everyday to class on time.

_____

_____

EXERCISE 2 (Do this exercise on your own. Then check your answers with a classmate.)

Directions: To practice correct word order for indirect questions, complete the following sentences using an indirect question.

Example: I wonder where _the chemistry building is._

---

1. The professor said he doesn't know when _____

_____

2. Your term paper does not cover how _____

_____

3. I'm sorry but I did not understand what _____

_____

EXERCISE 3 (Do this exercise with a classmate.)

Directions: The following paragraph has several errors in word order. First, read the paragraph, underlining any word-order problems. Then write the correct word order above each part you have underlined. The first error has been corrected for you.

Although you can learn vocabulary in your English class and from your textbooks, you may never have considered the many other handy reference tools that you can use to build up your vocabulary. Have you ever thought, for instance, what a great teacher the supermarket can be?

If you think about it, everything has either a label or a sign, making it
easy for you to connect <u>with the product the words</u>, *the words with the product* such as the words
chocolate chips on the label with a window on the package that lets you
see the chips, or a picture of diced tomatoes on a can. Besides, if you are
not still sure about what is a product, you can ask in the store another
customer to help you, and you will be practicing your spoken English
besides. Have you ever thought, too, what a great resource the Yellow
Pages of the telephone directory can be? If you look at the advertise-
ments, a wealth of words you can learn—all organized in specialized cate-
gories. Just consider, for example, what you can learn under *Pizzas.* You
can find ads for the different styles of pizzas and also learn just how many
different kinds of crusts are there. Many pizza places have in their ads
helpful pictures, and you can also learn some interesting mottoes, such as
"Fastest wheels west of the Rockies!" or "Only Chicago-style pizza in
Montana!" Even if you are not living in an English-speaking country,
many major libraries have telephone directories available so that you can
sit down and look at the Yellow Pages for, say, Chicago or New York.
Instead of throwing away those catalogs that come to your mailbox, have
you thought ever what an excellent resource they can be for words?
Because the buyer has to order sight unseen, the catalogs have excellent
pictures with detailed descriptions of the products. In a large mail-order
catalog, for example, you could learn what is a frost-free refrigerator or
what are the names of different golf clubs. In a catalog for clothes, you
could learn names exotic for colors and see the color itself illustrated. So,

the next time you complain about not knowing enough vocabulary, get out of the house and go to the supermarket, or if you insist on staying home, pick up your telephone directory or the latest catalog that in the mail came and get busy!

■ PART IV: Writing Activity

In Part IV, you will
- *plan and write a response to a selected topic*
- *share your writing with a classmate*
- *edit your writing for content and sentence-level accuracy*

Step 1—Choosing a Writing Topic

Select one or both of the following:

Topic A: Write about a custom from your culture or the United States that you find either desirable or undesirable. First, describe the custom. Then evaluate it in terms of how desirable or undesirable you think it is.

Topic B: Write about a problem in your home country or city or in the city in which you are currently living. First, explain the problem. In explaining it, you may wish to give the causes and/or the effects. Then suggest possible solutions. (**Note**: If you wish, you could choose to write on a problem you are facing personally.)

Step 2—Gathering Information

Once you have selected a topic, discuss it with a classmate or in a small group. If you have chosen Topic A, discuss a custom. Explain why you think it is desirable or undesirable. If you have chosen Topic B, discuss a problem, including its causes and effects. Discuss possible solutions to the problem.

Step 3—Prewriting

Working by yourself, list some of the ideas you have discussed with a classmate or in a small group. For Topic A, make notes on the custom, noting reasons why it is desirable or not. For Topic B, list the causes and/or effects of the problem you want to write about. List some solutions also.

Step 4—Writing Your First Draft

Use your list from prewriting to help you write your first draft. Focus on content.

Step 5—Sharing Your Draft

Working with a classmate, read each other's draft. Give feedback to each other using this format:

A. Reading for Content

1. What do you like most about this paper?
2. What would you still like to know more about?
3. What suggestions do you have for the writer?

B. Checking for Word-Order Errors

1. Put brackets [ ] around any sentences that contain word-order errors in your classmate's draft.
2. Discuss how to correct them.

Step 6—Revising Your Writing

Using your classmate's suggestions as well as your own ideas for revising, write your second draft. Focus on content and sentence-level accuracy. In particular, check for errors in word order.

Step 7—Proofreading Your Final Draft

Read your final draft once again, paying particular attention to word order. Make any necessary changes.

Postwriting Activity

Step 1—When your response is returned, check to see if your instructor has marked any errors in word order.

Step 2—If so, review the material in *Part II* of this unit.

Step 3—Correct each word-order error by rewriting the sentence that contains the error. If you are unsure of the correction, ask a classmate or your instructor for help.

■ PART V: Applying What You Have Learned to Other Writing Assignments

In Part V, you will

● *look for and correct word-order errors in any other writing assignments you have completed*

If you are in a composition class or another class in which you do writing, take your last returned paper and follow these directions:

1. Check whether your instructor has marked any word-order errors on your paper. If so, try to correct them using the material you have learned in this unit as a guide.

2. If your instructor has not marked any word-order errors on your paper, take one paragraph and check the word order of each sentence yourself. Try to determine if your word order is correct. If you are not sure, ask a classmate or your instructor to help you.

3. When you do writing assignments in the future, be sure to check for word-order errors.

UNIT 7: CONNECTOR*

*conn = grading symbol for connector errors

■ PART I: What You Need to Know About Connector Errors

> ### *In Part I, you will answer the following questions:*
> - *What is a connector error?*
> - *Why is it important to avoid connector errors in writing?*
> - *What are some strategies for mastering connectors?*

Definition of the Error

A connector error (**conn**) is an error in which the connection between words, clauses, sentences, or paragraphs is either unclear or illogical because of a doubled, missing, incorrect, or misplaced connector. The sentence *Even I studied the material for five hours, I still would not be ready for the test* has a connector error: the word *even* cannot connect the two clauses. The sentence should read: <u>*Even if*</u> *I studied the material for five hours, I still would not be ready for the test.*

A connector is a word, or sometimes a phrase, used to link paragraphs, sentences, clauses, or words. To understand connectors, you need to understand the types of clauses and connectors and the functions of each. The following two charts serve as a guide:

TYPES OF CLAUSES AND THEIR DEFINITIONS

Note: All clauses must have a subject and a verb.

An **independent clause** can stand alone as a sentence because its meaning is complete.

Example: Last year my university had an enrollment of 15 thousand.

A **dependent or subordinate clause** cannot stand alone but must work together with an independent clause to complete its meaning.

Example: Although last year my university had an enrollment of 15 thousand (dependent clause), this year the number of students has increased by ten percent (independent clause).

TYPES OF CONNECTORS AND THEIR FUNCTIONS

Coordinating conjunctions connect words, phrases, or independent clauses.

Examples: The students bought juice, soft drinks, <u>and</u> cookies for the party.

The dog ran out of the house <u>and</u> started chasing the car.

Tonight we can go to a movie <u>or</u> to a disco.

Pedro wanted to study engineering, <u>but</u> his father convinced him to study medicine. (Note that the two clauses have equal emphasis.)

Subordinating conjunctions connect a dependent (or subordinate) clause with an independent clause.

Example: <u>When</u> we have finished the chapter, we will have a test. (Note that the two clauses have unequal emphasis. The dependent clause is subordinate and thus has less emphasis.)

Correlative conjunctions connect similar grammatical structures.

Examples: You will have to <u>either</u> get a job <u>or</u> cut down on your expenses to stay in school.

Thuy <u>not only</u> has two classes today <u>but</u> she <u>also</u> has a term paper due.

Transitional words and phrases link sentences and link paragraphs.

Example: I dislike going to class at night; <u>however</u>, I cannot go during the day.

Importance of Mastering Connectors in Writing

Errors with connectors are global (more serious) errors and, as such, affect the meaning of whole sentences. Connectors are especially important because writers use them to show relationships between ideas, such as cause/effect, contrast, or a time sequence.

Connectors also enable writers to connect their ideas coherently. By providing smooth links between ideas, connectors help make writing clear and easy for the reader to follow.

Suggestions for Mastering Connectors

In order to use connectors skillfully, you must be certain of their meaning. The chart in this unit, arranged by meaning, serves as a reference you can consult to make sure that you are using the appropriate connector. Also, by becoming aware of how connectors have been used in the material that you read, you can improve your ability to use connectors correctly.

Part I, continued

TEST YOUR UNDERSTANDING OF CONNECTORS

After you have read *Part I*, write answers to the following questions. Share your answers with another student.

1. What is a connector? Explain in your own words.
2. What do connectors enable a writer to do?
3. Do you think about using connectors when you write? Explain your answer.
4. How can you improve your ability to use connectors?

■ PART II: Common Problems, Rules, and Self-help Strategies

In Part II, you will

- *study six problems ESL writers commonly have with connectors*
- *learn selected rules and self-help strategies for controlling errors with connectors*
- *learn the meaning of commonly used connectors*

This section contains six problems ESL writers commonly have with connectors. First, study each problem and the examples that illustrate it. Then mark the problems you think you have when you write in English. Remember that if you become aware of the type of connector errors you most often make, you will increase your chances of avoiding these errors in your writing.

PROBLEM I. Two connectors have been used where only one is needed.

	conn *conn*
Incorrect:	<u>Even though</u> my mother is trying to learn English, <u>but</u> she finds studying it difficult.
Correct:	<u>Even though</u> my mother is trying to learn English, she finds studying it difficult.
Correct:	My mother is trying to learn English, <u>but</u> she finds studying it difficult.

Self-help Strategy: Remember that a subordinating connector connects a dependent clause to an independent clause and a coordinating connector connects two independent clauses. In the preceding corrected sentences, note that you have the option of using either a subordinating or a coordinating connector, but not both.

PROBLEM 2. A connector is missing where it is needed.

Incorrect: I did not study; I got an A on the test.
> (These two clauses are grammatically correct, but without a connector, the reader cannot see how the ideas are connected.)

Incorrect: I did not study, I got an A on the test.
> (Two independent clauses cannot be connected with a comma.)

Correct: <u>Although</u> I did not study, I got an A on the test.

Correct: I did not study, <u>but</u> I got an A on the test.

Incorrect: Pedro was <u>so</u> happy when he heard the news he called Mexico.

Correct: Pedro was <u>so</u> happy when he heard the news <u>that</u> he called Mexico.

Incorrect: I frequently read magazines, go to the movies in my leisure time.

Correct: I frequently read magazines <u>and</u> go to the movies in my spare time.

Self-help Strategy: Always make sure that you use a connector to link two ideas when you need to show a relationship between them, even though the two ideas are in independent clauses. When using a connector that is more than one word, be sure to remember to include all the words.

PROBLEM 3. A connector with the wrong meaning has been used to join two clauses.

Incorrect: Bob refuses to wear a tie <u>while</u> the restaurant requires one.

Correct: Bob refuses to wear a tie <u>even though</u> the restaurant requires one.

> (*Even though* is needed to show a concession, establishing that despite the fact that the restaurant has this rule, Bob chooses not to follow it. *While is* used to show a contrast in ideas, rather than a concession, as in the sentence <u>*While* Kyle likes cats, *his sister Anna prefers dogs.*</u>)

Incorrect: I was very nervous about writing an essay in just one hour; <u>moreover</u>, I conquered my fears and finished the essay.

Correct: I was very nervous about writing an essay in just one hour; <u>however</u>, I conquered my fears and finished the essay.
> (*Moreover* adds information, as in the sentence *I am very tired right now;* <u>*moreover,*</u> *I am hungry. However* sets up a contrast.)

Self-help Strategy: Make sure the connector you have chosen gives the correct meaning to the sentence. Refer to *Commonly Used Connectors and Their Meanings* in this unit for a list of connectors and their meanings.

PROBLEM 4. The connector is correct but is with the wrong clause.

Incorrect: He broke the window <u>because</u> he had to pay for it.
conn (above "because")

Correct: <u>Because</u> he broke the window, he had to pay for it.

Self-help Strategy: Carefully consider the logical relationship that you want to establish between clauses so that you put the connector with the clause to which it belongs.

PROBLEM 5. A word that does not function as a connector has been used where a connector is needed.

Incorrect: <u>Especially</u> my aunt likes hamburgers, we always buy one for her.
Correct: <u>Because</u> my aunt likes hamburgers, we always buy one for her.
   (*Especially* is an adverb. **Example:** I am <u>especially</u> tired on Mondays.)

Self-help Strategy: Make sure that you always use a word that is a connector to show the relationship between two clauses. Refer to *Commonly Used Connectors and Their Meanings* in this unit for a list of connectors.

PROBLEM 6. A prepositional phrase has been used to connect two clauses.

Incorrect: Pierre could not travel to Mexico <u>because of</u> his visa did not permit him to do so.
Correct: Pierre could not travel to Mexico <u>because</u> his visa did not permit him to do so.
   (*Because of* is a prepositional phrase. **Example:** Marlene refused to raise her hand in class <u>because of</u> her shyness.)

Note: A prepositional phrase cannot be used in place of a conjunction to connect two clauses, but it can function as a transition to link one sentence to another. Prepositional phrases commonly used as transitional words are *in addition to, because of, in spite of, in contrast with, in contrast to,* and *in comparison with.*

Example: Dimitri broke his leg while skiing. <u>Because of his accident</u>, he has to use crutches.
   (*Because of his accident* connects information in the first sentence to new information in the following sentence.)

Guide to Using Connectors: Meaning and Punctuation

To use connectors correctly, you need to know not only their grammatical function but also their meaning. You also need to know how to punctuate connectors correctly. In the following sections you will learn the meaning of the most commonly used connectors and also rules for punctuating sentences with connectors.

Commonly Used Connectors and Their Meanings

CONNECTORS THAT ADD INFORMATION			
Coordinating Conjunctions	**Subordinating Conjunctions**	**Correlative Conjunctions**	**Transitional Words & Phrases**
and		not only . . . but also both . . . and	also besides moreover furthermore in addition

> Examples: We have seen the movie *Gone with the Wind* twice, <u>and</u> we plan to see it again.
> <u>Both</u> my brother <u>and</u> I know how to play tennis.
> Ahmed speaks Arabic, French, and English; <u>in addition</u>, he can read German.

CONNECTORS THAT GIVE AN EXAMPLE OR ILLUSTRATE A POINT			
Coordinating Conjunctions	**Subordinating Conjunctions**	**Correlative Conjunctions**	**Transitional Words & Phrases**
			for example for instance to illustrate specifically in particular

> Examples: I like to travel; <u>specifically</u>, I visit countries where I can practice my Spanish.
> <u>For example</u>, last summer I spent two weeks in Mexico.

CONNECTORS THAT SHOW A CONTRAST			
Coordinating Conjunctions	**Subordinating Conjunctions**	**Correlative Conjunctions**	**Transitional Words & Phrases**
but	while whereas		however in contrast conversely on the contrary on the other hand otherwise still instead

Examples: Bill received an A in his German class, <u>but</u> Antoinette got a B.
<u>Whereas</u> most students dislike dormitory food, William loves it.
We were supposed to be in class at 8:00 A.M. sharp; <u>however</u>, Barry arrived at 8:10.

CONNECTORS THAT SHOW A CONCESSION			
Coordinating Conjunctions	**Subordinating Conjunctions**	**Correlative Conjunctions**	**Transitional Words & Phrases**
yet	although even though though despite the fact that		nevertheless even so admittedly

Examples: Albert knows that he should take vitamins, <u>yet</u> he refuses to buy them.
<u>Although</u> Ernest hates most American food, he loves fried chicken.
I need to wear reading glasses; <u>nevertheless</u>, I hate how I look in them.

CONNECTORS THAT SHOW A SIMILARITY			
Coordinating Conjunctions	**Subordinating Conjunctions**	**Correlative Conjunctions**	**Transitional Words & Phrases**
			likewise similarly in the same way

Examples: Algebra was hard for me in high school; likewise, I find calculus difficult in college.

CONNECTORS THAT SHOW A RESULT			
Coordinating Conjunctions	**Subordinating Conjunctions**	**Correlative Conjunctions**	**Transitional Words & Phrases**
so	so . . . that such . . . that		accordingly as a result consequently as a consequence therefore thus

Examples: Hiroshi finally got all his verb tenses right in an essay, so he is very happy.

Hiroshi is so happy he got his verb tenses right in an essay that he is telling everyone.

Hiroshi got all his verb tenses right in an essay; as a result, he is happy.

CONNECTORS THAT GIVE A REASON OR CAUSE			
Coordinating Conjunctions	**Subordinating Conjunctions**	**Correlative Conjunctions**	**Transitional Words & Phrases**
for	because since		

Examples: Mr. Cross received a plaque, for he was elected teacher of the year.

Because he was elected teacher of the year, Mr. Cross received a plaque.

CONNECTORS THAT ESTABLISH TIME RELATIONSHIP OR ORDER			
Coordinating Conjunctions	**Subordinating Conjunctions**	**Correlative Conjunctions**	**Transitional Words & Phrases**
	after as soon as before when while until whenever as as long as		first second afterward finally in conclusion meanwhile previously next subsequently

Examples: <u>When</u> the semester is over, I will take a vacation.

Martin is now a student; <u>previously</u>, he was a sales representative for a pharmaceutical company.

CONNECTORS THAT SHOW A CONDITION			
Coordinating Conjunctions	**Subordinating Conjunctions**	**Correlative Conjunctions**	**Transitional Words & Phrases**
or	if even if unless when whenever	whether . . . or	

Examples: I have to get dressed quickly, <u>or</u> I will be late for the movies. (<u>or else</u> can also be used)

<u>If</u> you study hard enough, you should pass the test.

<u>Whether</u> she plans to accompany me <u>or</u> not, I still am going to the concert.

CONNECTORS THAT EXPLAIN OR EMPHASIZE			
Coordinating Conjunctions	**Subordinating Conjunctions**	**Correlative Conjunctions**	**Transitional Words & Phrases**
			in fact namely that is actually in other words

Examples: The bookstore sells greeting cards; <u>in fact</u>, they have the best selection in town.

I have to study all weekend; <u>in other words</u>, I am behind in my homework.

CONNECTORS THAT SHOW PURPOSE			
Coordinating Conjunctions	**Subordinating Conjunctions**	**Correlative Conjunctions**	**Transitional Words & Phrases**
	so that in order that		

Examples: I am saving my money <u>so that</u> I can go on an exciting vacation this summer.

CONNECTORS THAT GIVE A CHOICE OR ALTERNATIVE			
Coordinating Conjunctions	**Subordinating Conjunctions**	**Correlative Conjunctions**	**Transitional Words & Phrases**
or		either . . . or	

Examples: We can go to the beach, <u>or</u> we can go to the mountains.

You can <u>either</u> ride the bus <u>or</u> take the subway to get to my apartment.

CONNECTORS THAT INDICATE PLACE			
Coordinating Conjunctions	**Subordinating Conjunctions**	**Correlative Conjunctions**	**Transitional Words & Phrases**
	where wherever		

Example: <u>Wherever</u> I travel, I usually meet someone who can speak English.

Rules for Punctuating Connectors

Type: Coordinating Conjunctions

> *Rule:* Put a comma before a coordinating conjunction unless the two sentences it connects are very short.

Examples: A new shopping center has opened five blocks from my apartment, <u>and</u> I have noticed that it is offering a special discount to senior citizens.

The movie has started, <u>but</u> Jane has not arrived. (Note that the comma could be omitted.)

Type: Subordinating Conjunctions

> *Rules:* Put a comma after a subordinate clause that introduces a sentence.
> Do not use a comma before a subordinate clause that follows the independent clause. (Exceptions: *While, whereas, although, even though*, and *though* are usually separated from the independent clause with a comma.)

Examples: <u>While I was busy registering for my classes and buying my books</u>, my friend Kerry was enjoying her vacation in Canada.

The dog finally stopped barking <u>after his owner came home and fed him</u>.

Our town voted not to ban leaf blowers, <u>whereas most other towns in our area already have regulations against them</u>.

Type: Correlative Conjunctions

> *Rule:* Put a comma before the second correlative conjunction if it connects two clauses but not if it connects words or phrases.

Examples: Eric is <u>not only</u> an outstanding teacher, <u>but</u> he is <u>also</u> a gourmet cook.

The French bakery downtown sells <u>not only</u> crusty bread <u>but also</u> flaky pastries.

Type: Transitional Words and Phrases

> *Rules:* Put a semicolon before and a comma after a transitional word or phrase if you want to use it to connect two independent clauses.
>
> Put a comma after a transitional word or phrase if you want to use it to introduce an independent clause.
>
> Put commas before and after a transitional word or phrase within a clause.

Examples: The weather forecast for today was for cooler temperatures with a possibility of rain; <u>however,</u> the sun is shining brightly. <u>Nevertheless,</u> I am going to take my umbrella to work. As an extra precaution, <u>moreover,</u> I am going to wear my raincoat.

■ PART III: Exercises

> ## In Part III, you will practice
> - *recognizing and correcting connector errors in individual sentences*
> - *recognizing connectors and their meaning in a paragraph*
> - *testing your ability to use connectors correctly by sentence completion and production*
> - *identifying the function and meaning of connectors in a reading selection*

EXERCISE 1 (Do this exercise on your own. Then check your answers with a classmate.)

Directions: Test your ability to use connectors correctly by identifying and then correcting any errors with connectors. If a sentence is correct, write _C_ . If it is incorrect, write _I_ . Then underline the error and write the correction above it.

Example: _I_   All humans know they have to eat, <u>for</u> they can live.   *so that*

_C_   Because Sarah was angry at her brother, she couldn't think clearly.

_____ 1. Especially my sister is an accountant, she is very busy during tax time.

_____ 2. The supermarket closes at 10 P.M.; nevertheless, it opens at 6 A.M. if you need milk for breakfast.

_____ 3. Because he did not want to go to chemistry laboratory, he went any way.

_____ 4. Because a car is expensive, so I have not bought one.

_____ 5. Not only did Ann dislike the color of my dress, she did not like its style.

_____ 6. They couldn't buy any coffee for that the store wasn't open yet.

_____ 7. Even though I dislike fish, however I ate it at my friend's house to be polite.

_____ 8. Because I caught a cold, my mother left the window open.

_____9. If you are planning to buy a computer, talk to me first.

_____10. I went to the bank, I did not have any money.

EXERCISE 2 (Do this exercise with a classmate.)

Directions: Read the whole paragraph. Then circle each connector and discuss its type and meaning with your classmates. If you are unsure, refer to *Commonly Used Connectors and Their Meanings*. The first one has been done for you.

subordinating/result

Today's modern airport has (so) many services to offer travelers (that) it can resemble a city in itself. First, like all cities, it offers food. If you want to purchase something to eat, restaurants and snack bars abound, ranging from hot dog carts to sit-down restaurants. However, you might just want a little quick energy; in that event, you can buy either your favorite candy bar or a bag of chips from one of the many gift shops, which offer gifts, food, magazines, newspapers, and drugstore items. Second, like any city, the modern airport has entertainment. While waiting for your flight, you will have no problem entertaining yourself. Many airports now have a television area, but you could also read or perhaps browse among the paperbacks in the airport's bookstores. Moreover, some airports now have art exhibits on display. Of course, you can always entertain yourself just by watching people. Third, if you were unable to get all your shopping or errands done, modern airports have an array of shops and services, just like a mall in a city. For example, you can go to the bank or florist, buy clothes, or pick up last-minute gifts. Many airports in the United States now have gift shops selling products that are specialties of that state. In the Minneapolis airport, for instance, you can buy maple syrup and wild rice as well as Indian crafts. Not only do these items make thoughtful gifts but they also teach the tourist about the state. Lastly, if you want to arrive looking neat and clean or if you just want a pick-me-up, in many airports you can go to a unisex beauty salon. With everything that modern airports have to offer, waiting for a flight no longer needs to be boring.

EXERCISE 3 (Do this exercise on your own. Then check your answers with a classmate.)

Directions: Test your knowledge of the meaning of connectors by adding a clause to complete each sentence.

1. Although learning English can be a long and sometimes difficult process,

   _____

2. Michelle has difficulty with her pronunciation; for example, _____

   _____

3. Chi Fai speaks English with very little accent; however, _____

   _____

4. Learning English is so important to Michelle and Chi Fai that _____

   _____

5. In addition, Michelle and Chi Fai _____

   _____

EXERCISE 4 (Do this exercise on your own. Then check your answers with a classmate.)

Directions: Write six sentences, using a connector with a different meaning in each sentence. Choose these connectors from the list of commonly used connectors and their meanings. Be sure that you also understand the grammatical function of the connector.

1. _____

   _____

2. _____
   _____

3. _____
   _____

4. _____
   _____

5. _____
   _____

6. _____
   _____

EXERCISE 5 (Do this exercise on your own. Then check your answers with a classmate.)

Directions: Choose a short article in a newspaper or a magazine. Read the article. Then underline the connectors in two paragraphs and write down the function and meaning of each connector. Check your work with a classmate.

■ PART IV: Writing Activity

> **In Part IV, you will**
> - *plan and write a response to a selected topic*
> - *share your writing with a classmate*
> - *edit your writing for content and sentence-level accuracy*

Step 1—Choosing a Writing Topic

Select one or more of the following:

Topic A: Students always seem to discover a place where they feel they study or read best. What is your favorite place to study or read, and what makes it such a good place to study for you?

Topic B: Computers are in widespread use today in business and at home. What have been some of the major effects computers have had on our daily lives?

Topic C: Pretend that someone is going to visit your country or your hometown. That person has asked you how to get from the nearest airport to your town. Write a step-by-step description of how to get there. (As an alternate topic, you can tell a student in your class how to get to your house, apartment, or room.)

Topic D: Although most people see a college education as a good investment in the future, not everyone sees a college education as useful. What are some of the major benefits of a college education? When would a college education not be necessary or even desirable?

Topic E: Compare and contrast the person you are today with the person you were two years ago. What are the major changes in yourself and what has stayed the same ?

Step 2—Gathering Information

Once you have selected a topic, discuss it with a classmate or in a small group. If you have chosen Topic B, for example, discuss some of the major effects computers have had on our daily lives.

Step 3—Prewriting

Working by yourself, list some of the ideas you have discussed with a classmate or in a small group. Be sure to jot down some examples to illustrate your ideas.

Step 4—Writing Your First Draft

Use your list from prewriting to help you write your first draft. Focus on content.

Step 5—Sharing Your Draft

Working with a classmate, read each other's draft. Give feedback to each other by completing the following:

A.   Reading for Content
1. What did you like most about this paper?
2. What would you still like to know more about?
3. What suggestions do you have for the writer?

B.   Checking for Errors with Connectors
1 Circle any errors with connectors you notice on your classmate's draft.
2. Discuss how to correct them.

Step 6—Revising Your Writing

Using your classmate's suggestions as well as your own ideas for revising, write your second draft. Focus on content and sentence-level accuracy, looking in particular for any errors with connectors.

Step 7—Proofreading Your Final Draft

Read your final draft once again, paying particular attention to connectors. Make any necessary changes.

Postwriting Activity

Step 1—When your paper is returned, check to see if your instructor has marked any errors in using connectors.

Step 2—If so, review the material in *Part II* of this unit.

Step 3—Correct each connector error by rewriting the sentence that contains an error. If you are unsure of the answer, ask your instructor for help.

■ PART V: Applying What You Have Learned to Other Writing Assignments

In Part V, you will

- *look for and correct errors with connectors in any other writing assignments you have done*

If you are in a composition class or another class in which you do writing, take your last returned paper and do the following:

1. Check whether your instructor has marked any errors with connectors. If so, try to correct them, using the material you have learned in this unit as a guide.
2. If your instructor has not marked any errors with connectors, take one paragraph and underline any connectors. Try to determine whether the connectors are correct. If you are not sure, ask a classmate or your instructor to help you.
3. When you do writing assignments in the future, be sure to check for errors with connectors.

UNIT 8: PASSIVE*

*pass = grading symbol for errors with the passive

■ PART I: What You Need to Know About Errors with the Passive

> **In Part I, you will answer the following questions:**
> - *What is an error with the passive?*
> - *Why is it important to avoid errors with the passive in writing?*
> - *What are some strategies for mastering the passive?*

Definition of the Error

An error with the passive (**pass**) occurs when a verb in the passive voice has been incorrectly formed or when the passive voice has been used where the active voice is needed.

In English, a verb can be used in either the active voice or the passive voice. In the sentence *The bookstore _sells_ inexpensive notebooks,* the verb is in the active voice because the subject is doing the action. In the sentence *The computer shop _will be moved_ to temporary quarters this spring,* the verb is in the passive voice because the subject is being acted upon. The doer of the action is not named; "by someone" is understood. However, in the sentence *Our Spanish textbook _was written_ by my teacher,* the doer of the action—"by my teacher"—is named. The writer chooses whether or not to name the doer of the action depending on how important it is for the reader to have that information.

Even when the passive has been correctly formed in a sentence, a problem with the passive voice may still occur because the active voice may be preferable to the passive voice in that sentence. In that case, your instructor may use an alternative symbol, **wk pass** (for weak passive).

The verb *be* + the past participle, as in the sentence *The lake _is situated_ halfway between the two towns,* is sometimes considered a passive construction. Errors in this type of formation are treated in *Unit 14.*

Importance of Mastering the Passive in Writing

Knowing how to form the passive correctly is very important for an ESL writer. If the passive is incorrectly formed in a sentence, the reader will try to supply its correct form but may be confused about whether the writer intended to use the active voice or the passive voice.

The ESL writer also needs to know when to use the passive voice because such decisions can affect the style and clarity of a piece of writing. A writer, for example, might have to decide between *When I hear people speak Spanish* (active voice), *I think of my childhood in Mexico* and *When I hear Spanish being spoken* (passive voice), *I think of my childhood in Mexico.* Both sentences are grammatically correct, but in the first one the writer emphasizes the doer of the action (people) and in the second one what is acted upon (Spanish). However, a passive construction can sometimes make a sentence wordy which, of course, will negatively affect the writer's style. The sentence *It is stated by the author that Mondays are depressing,* in which the verb is in the passive voice, is wordy compared with the sentence *The author states that Mondays are depressing,* in which the verb is in the active voice.

In academic and professional writing, the writer uses both active and passive voice; therefore, it is essential that ESL writers master the formation and use of the passive voice.

Suggestions for Mastering the Passive

In order to avoid errors with the passive, a good strategy is to memorize how to form it so that you can do so automatically. Always remember to put the verb *to be* in the tense you need and then add the past participle to it. In the sentence *The winner will be chosen tonight,* the verb *to be* is in the future tense *(will be)* followed by the past participle of the verb *choose (chosen).* If you have any doubts about the formation of the passive voice in the tense you want to use, consult the chart in *Part II* of this unit.

If you are not sure whether the verb you have chosen can be used in the passive, check your ESL dictionary (or a standard dictionary) to find out whether or not the verb is transitive (takes a direct object and can be made passive, like the verbs *collect, teach,* or *follow*) or intransitive (does not take a direct object and cannot be made passive, like the verbs *arrive, exist,* or *stay*). However, the more skilled you are at knowing how to form the passive, the more you can rely on your own knowledge and not have to use reference books. You will thus be better prepared to control the passive in writing situations, such as exams, where you may not be allowed to use a dictionary or a grammar reference book.

Besides knowing how to form the passive voice correctly, you also need to know how to use it effectively. In expository writing, the active voice is generally a better choice than the passive voice except in cases where the writer wants to emphasize what has happened rather than who or what caused the action. In the sentence *The house was built in 1929,* for example, the emphasis is on the fact that the house was built rather than on who built it. Most importantly, the ESL writer must remember that ineffective use of the passive can cause problems with focus in a paragraph and make it difficult for the reader to follow what the writer is saying. You will see this problem illustrated in *Part II* of this unit.

In scientific writing, the passive voice is often preferred. If you need to write a scientific paper or a laboratory report, a good strategy you can use to determine to what extent you need to use the passive voice is to examine similar papers in that field or any sample papers the instructor has provided so that you can see the balance of active and passive voice. If you are in doubt, ask your instructor for help.

Another strategy for mastering the use of the active and passive voice is to compare the way the two voices are used when you are reading textbooks, the newspaper, or magazine articles. In particular, try to determine why the author used the passive instead of the active voice and whether or not you think its use is effective.

TEST YOUR UNDERSTANDING OF THE PASSIVE

After you have read *Part I*, write answers to the following questions. Share your answers with another student.

1. What is the difference between passive and active voice?
2. What two things does a writer have to know about the passive to use it correctly?
3. Do you ever avoid using the passive when you write? Explain your answer.
4. How can you improve your ability to use the passive?

■ PART II: Common Problems, Rules, and Self-help Strategies

In **Part II,** *you will*

- *study four problems ESL writers commonly have with the passive*
- *learn self-help strategies and selected rules for controlling the passive*
- *review how to form the passive*

This section presents four problems ESL writers commonly have with the passive. First, study each problem and the examples that illustrate it. Then mark the problems you think you have when you write in English. Remember that if you become aware of the type of errors you most often make with the passive, you will increase your chances of avoiding these errors in your writing.

PROBLEM 1. **The passive has been incorrectly formed.**

Incorrect: Some pronunciation problems ca̲n̲ ̲b̲e̲ ̲f̲i̲x̲ easily. *(pass)*

Correct: Some pronunciation problems c̲a̲n̲ ̲b̲e̲ ̲f̲i̲x̲e̲d̲ easily.

Incorrect: Your grades w̲i̲l̲l̲ ̲s̲e̲n̲t̲ next week. *(pass)*

Incorrect: Your grades w̲i̲l̲l̲ ̲b̲e̲i̲n̲g̲ ̲s̲e̲n̲t̲ next week. *(pass)*

Correct: Your grades w̲i̲l̲l̲ ̲b̲e̲ ̲s̲e̲n̲t̲ next week.

Self-help Strategy: Refer to the chart in this section to see if you have formed the passive correctly in the verb tense you are using.

PROBLEM 2. **The passive voice is needed instead of the active voice.**

Incorrect: A new air conditioner i̲n̲s̲t̲a̲l̲l̲ next week. *(pass)*

Correct: A new air conditioner w̲i̲l̲l̲ ̲b̲e̲ ̲i̲n̲s̲t̲a̲l̲l̲e̲d̲ next week. (The air conditioner cannot install itself but must be installed by someone.)

Self-help Strategy: Always remember that if the subject is doing the action, you should use the active voice. If the action is being done to the subject by someone or something, you should use the passive voice.

PROBLEM 3. **The passive voice has been used with a verb that cannot be made passive.**

Incorrect: Male dominance over females still i̲s̲ ̲e̲x̲i̲s̲t̲e̲d̲ in some countries. *(pass)*

Correct: Male dominance over females still e̲x̲i̲s̲t̲s̲ in some countries.

Incorrect: A power failure w̲a̲s̲ ̲o̲c̲c̲u̲r̲r̲e̲d̲ last month. *(pass)*

Correct: A power failure o̲c̲c̲u̲r̲r̲e̲d̲ last month.

Rule: Only transitive verbs, verbs that can take a direct object, can be made passive. Intransitive verbs, verbs that cannot take a direct object, cannot be made passive.

Self-help Strategy: If you are unsure whether a verb is transitive or intransitive, check the verb in a dictionary.

PROBLEM 4. **The passive voice has been used where the active voice would be more effective.**

Note: Although this problem is probably more common to native speakers than to ESL writers, you still need to be aware of ineffective use of the passive voice. An alternate symbol for this kind of problem with the passive is **wk pass**—weak passive. (The weak passive is treated in composition textbooks for native speakers.)

Ineffective Use of the Passive Voice

In the following short paragraph, the passive voice has been used inef-
fectively. There is no focus on who had the problem with organization
or what the weakness was.

Listing my ideas in an unorganized form is a second weakness of mine
in writing. Organization <u>was</u> not adequately <u>taught</u> *pass* by high school. My
thoughts <u>were scribbled</u> *pass* in list form and <u>were accepted</u> *pass* by my
instructors.

Revised Paragraph with the Active Voice

In the revised paragraph below, the writer uses the active voice, and the
focus of the paragraph revolves around how the writer wrote in a disorganized fashion.

Listing my ideas in an unorganized form is a second weakness of mine
in writing. My high school English teachers did not adequately teach
organization. Instead of following a prescribed method of prewriting like
brainstorming or clustering, I merely scribbled out my thoughts in list
form and my instructors accepted them.

Self-help Strategy: Use the active voice unless you have a good reason to
use the passive voice.

Guide to Forming the Passive

Passive of Verb Tenses

The passive is formed by using the form of the helping verb *to be* in whatever tense the writer selects and then adding the past participle.

Verb-Tense Formation in Passive Voice	Example
Present am, is, are + past participle	Mail <u>is delivered</u> to the residence hall every day except Sunday.
Present progressive am being, is being, are being + past participle	A new addition <u>is being added</u> to the library.
Past was, were + past participle	The grades <u>were posted</u> by the teaching assistant at 3:00 P.M.
Past progressive was being, were being + past participle	When I arrived at Wellman Hall, the corrected problem sets <u>were</u> just <u>being distributed.</u>
Past Perfect has been, have been + past participle	I think the money <u>has</u> already <u>been sent</u> electronically by the bank.
Past Perfect had been + past participle	All the food <u>had been eaten</u> when I arrived at the potluck.
Future will be + past participle	The tests <u>will be given back</u> on Thursday.
Future Perfect will have been + past participle	By the time you arrive at the concert hall, all the free tickets will <u>have been given</u> out.

Passive of Modal Verb Phrases

In a modal verb phrase, the passive is formed by adding *be* + the past participle after the modal for the present tense and *have been* + the past participle after the modal for the past tense.

Modal Verb-Tense Formation in Passive Voice	Example
Present modal + be + past participle	Revision for spelling <u>can</u> easily <u>be done</u> on a computer. Cheating on tests <u>should be reported</u> to the Judicial Board.
Past modal + have been + past participle	It is possible that the train <u>could have been delayed</u>. I think she <u>should have been elected</u> chair of the committee.

Passive of Conditional Verb Phrases

In a conditional sentence, the passive can be used in either the condition clause or the result clause, or in both. To correctly form the passive of the conditional verb phrase, use the guides to forming the passive of verb tenses and modal verb phrases in this section. The chart below shows examples of the passive voice in conditional sentences.

Conditional Verb-Phrase Formation in Passive Voice	Example
Note: Use the passive of the appropriate verb tense or modal verb phrase.	
Real conditional	If Ben makes a mistake, he <u>is corrected</u> by his friend.
Hypothetical conditional (present or future)	If the computer software were <u>shipped</u> tonight, it would arrive tomorrow. (<u>was</u> becomes <u>were</u> in the *if* clause)
Hypothetical conditional (past)	If the dam <u>had</u> not <u>been constructed</u>, we would have had a flood last spring.

Passive of Infinitives and Gerunds

Infinitives in Passive Voice	Example
Present infinitive to + be + past participle	She arranged for the make-up test <u>to be given</u> Monday.
Perfect infinitive to + have been + past participle	The results were supposed <u>to have been sent</u> yesterday.

Gerunds in Passive Voice	Example
being + past participle	He did not like <u>being called</u> Jim instead of James. <u>Being awakened</u> in the middle of the night by a telephone call upset George. After <u>being told</u> to go from one office to another, Phil finally found where to turn in his financial aid forms.

■ PART III: Exercises

> ## In Part III, you will practice
> - forming the passive correctly
> - recognizing and correcting errors with the passive in individual sentences
> - recognizing the passive and why it has been used in a paragraph

EXERCISE I (Do this exercise on your own. Then check your answers with a classmate.)

Directions: Change the underlined verbs or verbals in the following sentences from the active voice to the passive voice, if possible. Make other changes in the sentences as necessary. Be particularly careful to use the correct formation of the passive for the verb tense you are using. If you are not sure, consult the charts in *Part II*.

When you check your answers with a classmate, discuss which sentence you prefer—the one with the verb in the active voice or the one with the verb in the passive voice. Take into consideration such things as which sentence is wordier, whether one sounds awkward, or whether who is doing the action is important.

Example: The Red Cross <u>collected</u> canned food and clothes for the earthquake victims.

Canned food and clothing <u>were collected</u> for the earthquake victims by the Red Cross.

Note: The sentence in the active voice is less wordy, but if the writer wants to emphasize what was collected by the Red Cross, the sentence in the passive voice should be used.

---

1. Most restaurants <u>accept</u> credit cards.

_____

_____

2. They <u>must have moved</u> the bookstore since I was last here.

_____

_____

3. The teacher expects the students <u>to do</u> the assignment before the next class.

_____

_____

4. If the temperature had dropped last night, snow <u>would have fallen</u>.

_____

_____

5. The anchor <u>interrupted</u> the program for a special news bulletin.

_____

_____

6. By the time I get home, the letter carrier <u>will have delivered</u> the mail.

_____

_____

7. At the end of the school year, teachers and students <u>are</u> ready for summer vacation.

_____

_____

8. The university press <u>has published</u> Dr. Robertson's book.

_____

_____

9. The dog did not like <u>moving</u> from one house to another.

_____

_____

10. Although I <u>had expected</u> six people for dinner, ten showed up.

_____

_____

EXERCISE 2 (Do this exercise on your own. Then check your answers with a classmate.)

Directions: All sentences contain errors with the passive. Test your knowledge of the formation and use of the passive by underlining the error and then rewriting the sentence correctly.

Example: When I was walking in the streets of Taiwan, Chinese <u>was speaking</u> all around me.

When I was walking in the streets of Taiwan, Chinese was being spoken all around me.

---

1. We constantly being asked by the government for more taxes.

_____

_____

2. My conversation with her conducted in Vietnamese.

_____

_____

3. Are you sure that company is still existed?

_____

_____

4. Juan has the honor of having awarded the prize for the best attendance.

_____

_____

5. A solid friendship create between them because of their common interest in soccer.

_____

_____

6. My fear about speaking English in public was contributed to my shyness.

_____

_____

7. This English class offers only to nonnative speakers.

_____

_____

8. When the announcement was been made, some students were not there.

_____

_____

9. Some English words derived from Latin.

_____

_____

EXERCISE 3 (Do this exercise with a classmate.)

Directions: The writer of this paragraph has elected to use some verbs in the passive. The paragraph, as written, works well. Read the whole paragraph. Then underline each verb or verbal in the passive voice. With your classmate, discuss whether or not you might want to make any changes from the passive to the active. The first one has been done for you.

                                      passive

Although riding the train <u>has been</u> negatively <u>labeled</u> as nostalgic in our car-dependent society and many trains have long ceased to exist, a short commuter train ride can be a unique trip into the past—and a beautiful ride. On a recent short train trip, I was thrilled by the variety of bird life in the salt marsh the train passed through. In fact, the train was virtually ignored by the stately white egrets, shiny red-winged blackbirds, and plump mallard ducks. As we moved out of the marsh and glided along the water's edge, we were greeted by the fishermen out to try their luck for the day. Farther from shore lay the oil tankers, and behind them in the distance the bay was decorated with white sails. As we approached the city, I wondered if there was anything left to be seen. To my surprise, I found myself looking into people's backyards, catching glimpses of downtown streets, and, best of all, being treated to a panoramic view of the highway. There cars were creeping along, bumper to bumper, while out on the tracks, we peacefully glided by, rocking gently on the rails. I like to think that as our whistle tooted, it may have been heard by a driver out there who wished he or she were on the train.

■ PART IV: Writing Activity

> ### *In Part IV, you will*
> - *plan and write a response to a selected topic*
> - *share your writing with a classmate*
> - *edit your writing for content and sentence-level accuracy*

Step 1—Choosing a Writing Topic

Select one or more of the following:

Topic A: What has been discovered in the last two decades and how, in your opinion, has it benefited people?

Topic B: Now that computers are so widely used in the workplace, it has been suggested that some workers would not have to go to the job but could work at home via computer. Would you consider taking such a job if it were offered to you?

Step 2—Gathering Information

Work with a classmate or in a small group. If you have chosen Topic A, discuss some recent discoveries. Decide which one you would like to write about and then tell why you have chosen it. If you have chosen Topic B, discuss what it would be like to work at home via computer and give reasons for or against such a job.

Step 3—Prewriting

Work by yourself. For Topic A, list ways in which the discovery has benefited people. Also, include how it has enriched your life. For Topic B, list two or three reasons for or against working at home via computer. Jot down examples that will illustrate your points.

Step 4—Writing Your First Draft

Use your notes to help you write your draft. Focus on content.

Step 5—Sharing Your Draft

Working with a classmate, read each other's draft. Give feedback to each other by completing the following:

A. **Reading for Content**
1. What did you like most about this piece of writing?
2. What would you still like to know more about?
3. What suggestions do you have for the writer?

B. **Checking for Errors with Connectors**
1. Circle any errors with connectors on your classmate's draft.
2. Discuss how to correct them.

Step 6—Revising Your Writing

Using your classmate's suggestions as well as your own ideas, write your second draft. Focus on content and sentence-level accuracy, paying special attention to how you have used the passive voice.

Step 7—Proofreading Your Final Draft

Read your final draft once again. Make necessary changes.

Postwriting Activity

Step 1—Check if your instructor has marked any errors in using the passive.

Step 2—If so, review the material in *Part II* of this unit.

Step 3—Fix each error with the passive by rewriting the sentence correctly.

■ PART V: Applying What You Have Learned to Other Writing Assignments

In* Part V, *you will

- *look for and correct errors with the passive in other writing*

If you are in a composition class or another class in which you do writing, take your last returned paper and follow these directions:

1. Check whether your instructor has marked any errors with the passive. If so, try to correct them, using the material you have learned in this unit.
2. If your instructor has not marked any errors with the passive, take one paragraph and underline each verb or verb phrase. If you have used the passive voice, check to see if you have formed it correctly and decide whether or not the active voice would have been more effective.
3. When you are writing in the future, check for errors with the passive.

UNIT 9: UNCLEAR*

*unclear = grading symbol for unclear sentences

■ PART I: What You Need to Know About Unclear Sentences

In Part I, you will answer the following questions:

- What is an unclear sentence?
- Why is it important to avoid unclear sentences in writing?
- What are some strategies for mastering sentence clarity?

Definition of the Error

In an unclear (**unclear**) sentence, the reader cannot understand the message the writer wants to convey. The error is global (more serious) because it affects more than a clause and may affect whole parts of a text.

An unclear message may or may not be related to problems with grammar in a sentence. For example, unclear sentences like *Pressure is one of equipment to bring up our skill by ourself* or *I can experienced the truth of studying by a coffee* are grammatically incorrect and have an unclear message. On the other hand, unclear sentences like *Waiting for these negatives to grow is not a particle way* or *I felt sick that I missed some tasteful water* are correct grammatically but their message is unclear. In an unclear sentence, the whole sentence or just part of the sentence may be unclear.

Unclear sentences differ from sentences with sentence-structure errors or sentences that are nonidiomatic because the meaning of these sentences is usually understandable, whereas the message of an unclear sentence is not clear to the reader.

Importance of Mastering Sentence Clarity in Writing

In academic and professional writing, the reader should not have to guess at meaning. However, in an unclear sentence, the reader must try to guess what the writer is saying—without the presence of the writer. This error is particularly serious as it interferes with the reader's ability to understand the content of a piece of writing. In other words, the meaning of the text is at least partially lost.

Suggestions for Mastering Sentence Clarity

Often, writers who can write quite easily and correctly about their own personal experiences find themselves writing unclear sentences when they begin writing on more abstract topics in academic or professional writing. A good strategy for becoming familiar with the language you will need to use and with the kinds of writing you will have to do in either academic or professional writing is to read examples of this kind of writing in textbooks, journals, newspapers, or magazines.

Remember that you, as the writer, have the responsibility for conveying your ideas clearly to the reader. The following are five strategies that will help you write clear sentences:

1. Avoid translating from your native language. Try to think and write in English as much as possible.

2. If you are having trouble expressing an idea in writing, try telling it to a classmate or your teacher. Then write it the way you said it. Do not worry that your English is "too simple." Being clear is more important than sounding sophisticated.

3. Use words that you know rather than "big words" whose meanings you are unsure of. You can then refine your language in later drafts of a paper. You will also find that as you gain more confidence in your writing skills, you will improve your command of words.

4. If a sentence on your paper has been marked *unclear*, you can try to rewrite it yourself. Rethink the idea you want to express, determine what you really want to say, and then restate the sentence.

5. When you are writing a draft and are in the process of formulating your ideas, do not be afraid to write some short, simple sentences to clarify your meaning to yourself. Then in later drafts you can combine some of these ideas into more complex sentences.

TEST YOUR UNDERSTANDING OF UNCLEAR SENTENCES

After you have read *Part I*, write answers to the following questions. Share your answers with another student.

1. What is an unclear sentence? Explain in your own words.

2. What makes an unclear sentence a particularly serious error?

3. Do you think you sometimes write unclear sentences?

4. Which strategies might best help you write clear sentences? Can you suggest other strategies that might work for you?

■ PART II: Examples of Unclear Sentences

The following examples of four unclear sentences are taken from students' writing. A correct version of the sentence has not been given because the meaning of the sentence is unclear and thus its message cannot be determined by anyone except the writer. Only the writer knows what he or she wanted to say and, therefore, only the writer can rewrite the sentence.

Incorrect: She seemingly see an edge of future's door to step in a brighter for her own.

Incorrect: Owing to the fact that the size of 18-year-old young people is shrinking, the influx of the labor force will compensate the lack of manpower of national services.

Incorrect: It is not easy improving a better life for everybody unless they have an academic.

Incorrect: He sees the achievement in alignment with extra effort put forth by his students had necessary to have extra office hours.

Notice how the unclear sentences in the following passage take away from its effectiveness because a whole piece of meaning is lost to the reader.

An example of how car decorations can identify us is a stuffed toy, which is often stuck on the car's windshield. These toys bring a car to people's attention, and therefore people from other cars [can know what *unclear* our message is], even at a very fast speed. [These toys mostly show that *unclear* person really the car and animals.]

■ PART III: Exercise

To see how well you can recognize unclear sentences in English, do the exercise below.

EXERCISE: (Do this exercise with a classmate.)

Directions: This paragraph, which was written by a student, has been edited so that the only errors are unclear sentences. Read the paragraph out loud to each other and listen for unclear sentences. Put between brackets any unclear sentences or parts of sentences you hear. Then read the paragraph to check it again for unclear sentences. Try to rewrite the unclear sentences to make them clear. Be prepared to discuss how easy or difficult it is to revise the unclear sentences of another writer.

There are many differences between third-world and industrialized nations. One important difference is in the types of worries individuals have in their daily lives. All human have worries but one hard tension for some people may differ hardness other people. In many parts of the world, people never think about buying new clothes or the latest model TV set or car. All that they think about is how they can get a food from hunger. People have a great terror and this thing has a lot of tension. In contrast, people who live in wealthy nations usually never think about food except where or when they are going to eat, but they have different problems in their lives, such as too much work, family problems, and stress. In both types of countries, rich and poor, people are never free from worry.

UNIT 10: SUBJECT–VERB AGREEMENT*

*sv = grading symbol for errors in subject-verb agreement

■ PART I: What You Need to Know About Errors in Subject-Verb Agreement

> **In Part I, you will answer the following questions:**
> - *What is an error in subject-verb agreement?*
> - *Why is it important to avoid subject-verb agreement errors in writing?*
> - *What are some strategies for mastering subject-verb agreement?*

Definition of the Error

A subject-verb agreement error (**sv**) is an error in which the form of a verb does not fit grammatically with the subject. For example, *she have* and *he see* illustrate errors in subject-verb agreement. *She have* should be *she has*, while *he see* should be *he sees*.

Importance of Mastering Subject-Verb Agreement in Writing

Subject-verb agreement errors are local (less serious) errors. Although a reader can still understand the meaning of a text even if it contains several subject-verb agreement errors, these errors will be highly noticeable and distracting. More importantly, readers in the academic and professional worlds expect writers to be able to use correct subject-verb agreement.

Suggestions for Mastering Subject-Verb Agreement

The rules for subject-verb agreement are relatively easy to master. If you tend to make this kind of error, first study the rules covered in this unit. Then check your writing for agreement errors by looking carefully at each subject and verb to see if they agree. In particular, be sure to check subject-verb agreement when several words appear between the subject and verb.

TEST YOUR UNDERSTANDING OF SUBJECT-VERB AGREEMENT

After you have read *Part I*, write answers to the following questions. Share your answers with another student.

1. What is a subject-verb agreement error? Explain in your own words.
2. How serious are subject-verb agreement errors?
3. Do you tend to make subject-verb agreement errors when you write in English?
4. What is one strategy ESL writers can use to master subject-verb agreement in their writing?

■ PART II: Common Problems, Rules, and Self-help Strategies

In Part II, you will

- *study six problems ESL writers commonly have with subject-verb agreement*
- *learn selected rules and self-help strategies for avoiding subject-verb agreement errors*

This section presents six problems ESL writers commonly have with subject-verb agreement. First, study each problem and the examples that illustrate it. Then mark the problems you think you have when you write in English. Remember that if you become aware of the type of errors in subject-verb agreement you most often make, you will increase your chances of avoiding these errors in your writing.

PROBLEM 1. The third-person singular has been incorrectly formed in the present tense.

Incorrect: Each spring the doctor <u>tell</u> my father to take a vacation.

Correct: Each spring the doctor <u>tells</u> my father to take a vacation.

Basic Rules for Subject-Verb Agreement

1. In the present tense, a third-person singular subject takes a verb that ends in *-s* or *-es*. The third-person singular includes the pronouns *he, she,* and *it,* as well as all other singular subjects, such as *the doctor, the dog,* and *the athlete.*

   Incorrect: Marta SV <u>work</u> as a bagger at the grocery store.
   Correct: Marta <u>works</u> as a bagger at the grocery store.

   Incorrect: My back SV <u>hurt</u>.
   Correct: My back <u>hurts</u>.

2. All other pronouns (*I, you, we, they*) and plural subjects, such as *books* or *classes,* do not take a verb ending in *-s.*

   Incorrect: Many students <u>chooses</u> sports to stay in shape.
   Correct: Many students <u>choose</u> sports to stay in shape.

   Incorrect: Her children <u>has</u> many different kinds of toys.
   Correct: Her children <u>have</u> many different kinds of toys.

3. A few nouns that end in *-s* are actually singular. Some of these include *sports, news,* and some fields of study *(physics, mathematics, economics).*

   Incorrect: Economics <u>are</u> a very interesting field of study.
   Correct: Economics <u>is</u> a very interesting field of study.

   Incorrect: The news <u>begin</u> at 6:00 P.M.
   Correct: The news <u>begins</u> at 6:00 P.M.

4. **The commonly used noun *people* is a collective noun and takes a plural verb.**

   Incorrect: The people going on the trip <u>is</u> already here.
   Correct: The people going on the trip <u>are</u> already here.

5. Uncountable nouns take a singular verb.

   Incorrect: The money <u>are</u> in the wallet.
   Correct: The money <u>is</u> in the wallet.

Note: Most errors in subject-verb agreement involve verbs in the present tense. However, subject-verb agreement errors also sometimes occur with the verb *to be* in the past tense.

   Incorrect: I <u>were</u> a student for four years.
   Correct: I <u>was</u> a student for four years.

   Incorrect: Max <u>were</u> a student for four years.
   Correct: Max <u>was</u> a student for four years.

Incorrect: Tomas and Blanca <u>was</u> students for four years. [SV]

Correct: Tomas and Blanca <u>were</u> students for four years.

Incorrect: We <u>was</u> students for four years. [SV]

Correct: We <u>were</u> students for four years.

PROBLEM 2. The subject and verb do not agree when words come between them.

Incorrect: Susan's lack of friends and relatives <u>make</u> her feel isolated. [SV]

Correct: Susan's lack of friends and relatives <u>makes</u> her feel isolated.

Self-help Strategy: Remember that words that appear between the subject and the verb do not affect agreement. In the example sentence above, the subject is *lack*; thus, the verb must take the third-person singular form, *makes.*

PROBLEM 3. The verb in a relative clause (sometimes called an adjective clause) does not agree with the noun that the clause modifies.

Incorrect: Every person should try to choose a place to live that <u>suit</u> his or her needs.   *relative clause* [SV]

Correct: Every person should choose a place to live that <u>suits</u> his or her needs.

Incorrect: The president, who <u>serve</u> a four-year term, lives in the White House.   *relative clause* [SV]

Correct: The president, who <u>serves</u> a four-year term, lives in the White House.

Self-help Strategy: Keep in mind that the verb in a relative clause always agrees with the word the relative pronoun (*that, which, who, whose, whom*) refers to. In the first example sentence, the verb in the relative clause must agree with the noun *place*. In the second sentence, it must agree with the noun *president*.

PROBLEM 4. The subject and verb do not agree when a gerund or infinitive is the subject of the verb.

Incorrect: <u>Being</u> a workaholic <u>have</u> many disadvantages. *gerund* [SV]

Correct: <u>Being</u> a workaholic <u>has</u> many disadvantages.

Incorrect: <u>To copy</u> someone else's answers on tests <u>are</u> wrong. *infinitive* [SV]

Correct: <u>To copy</u> someone else's answers on tests <u>is</u> wrong.

Self-help Strategy: Remember that when a gerund or an infinitive serves as a subject of a sentence, the verb connected with this subject will be in the singular form.

PROBLEM 5. The subject and verb do not agree when the clause or sentence begins with *there is* or *there are*.

Incorrect: There are a new car parked in my driveway.

Correct: There is a new car parked in my driveway. (The true subject is *a new car.*)

Incorrect: There is ten students in my discussion class.

Correct: There are ten students in my discussion class. (The true subject is *ten students.*)

Self-help Strategy: When using *there*, think ahead to the true subject, which follows the verb *to be*, so that you choose the correct form of the verb to agree with this true subject. Review the rules that follow on subject-verb agreement with *there*.

Rules for Subject-Verb Agreement with *There*

When a sentence or clause begins with *there*, the verb agrees with the true subject, which follows the verb.

1. *There is* is used before a singular or uncountable subject.

   Examples: There is enough air in my tires.
   There is a new book on the bestseller list.

2. *There are* is used before a plural subject.

   Examples: There are two new books on the bestseller list.
   There are three classes in physics being offered this semester.

3. When *there* is followed by a compound subject (two noun phrases joined by *and*), the verb agrees with the noun immediately following it.

   Examples: There is a new stereo and a new tape deck in her room.
   There are new twin beds and a CD player in her room.

PROBLEM 6. The subject and verb do not agree following the words *one of the*.

Incorrect: One of the students play the drums.

Correct: One of the students plays the drums.

Self-help Strategy: Keep in mind that even though the group of words *one of the* is always followed by a plural noun, the verb must agree with *one*, which is the true subject of the sentence.

■ PART III: Exercises

> **In Part III, you will practice**
> ● recognizing and correcting errors in subject-verb agreement in individual sentences
> ● recognizing and correcting errors in subject-verb agreement in a paragraph
> ● practicing correct subject-verb agreement in a paragraph

EXERCISE I (Do this exercise on your own. Then check your answers with a classmate.)

Directions: Using the material you have just studied in this unit as a guide, identify and correct any problems with subject-verb agreement in the following sentences. First, decide whether a sentence is correct (C) or incorrect (I). Then cross out and correct the incorrect verbs.

> Example: __I__ A student in the Netherlands usually ~~learn~~ *learns* to speak English, French, and German in school.

_____1. Marta's children is certainly well-behaved.

_____2. Physics is a popular major at my university.

_____3. Matthew, who is in second grade, already know how to read and write.

_____4. One of the students in the class was selected to participate in the essay contest.

_____5. If a child in China perform well enough in his or her sport, the child will have a chance to receive professional training.

_____6. Parents usually wants the best for their children.

_____7. Brainstorming help a writer to gather ideas and avoid writer's block.

_____8. There is several stages in the writing process, including prewriting, writing a draft, and revising.

_____9. Because of the drought, there are not enough water for all the farmers who need it.

EXERCISE 2 (Do this exercise on your own. Then check your answers with a classmate.)

Directions: Fill in each blank space with the correct form of the verb in parentheses. This paragraph, which was written by a student, is in the present tense.

My English class (differ) ____*differs*____ from my chemistry class in terms of the student-teacher relationship. With the small number of students in English 22, the relationship between the teacher and the students (be) _____ much closer than that of the teacher and students in Chemistry 1B. Since there (be) _____ only 12 students in English 22, the students (find) _____ it extremely easy to talk to their teacher one-on-one. At the beginning of every class on Mondays and Wednesdays from 2 to 4 P.M., I always (have) _____ something to say to my teacher, Lisa—either a question to ask her or a simple "hello." Also, since the class is small, Lisa always (walk) _____ around during class to help us with our specific problems, and she always (have) _____ time for a short conversation with each of us. Being able to get attention from the teacher in this way (help) _____ the students build a strong working relationship with their teacher. In contrast, since Chemistry 1B is such a large class, there (be) _____ very little chance for close student-teacher interaction. With about 500 students in her class, Dr. Ward rarely (answer) _____ individual students' questions in class. In fact, she is so busy even during her office hours that I (have) _____ not been able to ask her any questions all semester. Because of this lack of communication between Dr. Ward and the students, Chemistry 1B (have) _____ been more stressful for me than English 22.

EXERCISE 3 (Do this exercise with a classmate.)

Directions: The following paragraph contains some errors in subject-verb agreement. Cross out each incorrect verb and write the correct form above it.

April 15 is a well-known date in the United States. Every year on this day, everyone who work must file his or her income-tax forms with both the federal and state governments. Filing these forms are no easy task. First, a person needs to decide which forms to file. For federal income taxes, there is a long form for people who wishes to itemize their deductions. This form have at least five supplementary parts, called "schedules," and a person must decide which of these, if any, to file as well. Then there is a short form for people who plans to take the "standard" deduction, one that have been precalculated and is the same for everyone. The state income-tax forms are separate forms, and these must also be filed. In California, there is at least four supplementary schedules that a person may need to fill out. Once a person know which ones to file, completing all of these forms are not easy either, and many people hires an accountant to help them. Regardless of whether a taxpayer choose to complete the forms on his or her own or to seek assistance, the forms must be postmarked before midnight on April 15. This day is one of the busiest for the U.S. Postal Service since many taxpayers find themselves finishing the whole process at the last minute.

■ PART IV: Writing Activity

In Part IV, you will
- *plan and write a response to a given topic*
- *share your writing with a classmate*
- *edit your writing for content and sentence-level accuracy*

Step 1—Choosing a Writing Topic

Select one or both of the following:

Topic A: Write about a common expression or saying from your own culture or from the United States. First, explain what the saying means. Then explain whether or not you agree with it and why.

Topic B: Some people feel that we should continue space exploration, while others feel that doing so is too costly to be worthwhile. Write about whether or not the continuation of space exploration is important. Give reasons to support your point of view.

Step 2—Gathering Information

Once you have selected a topic, discuss it with a classmate or in a small group. If you have chosen Topic A, discuss the saying. Explain what it means and whether or not you agree with it. If you have selected Topic B, discuss some of the pros and cons of space exploration. Discuss how important you believe space exploration is.

Step 3—Prewriting

Working by yourself, list some of the ideas you have discussed with a classmate or in a group. For Topic A, make notes on what the saying you have chosen means. Jot down whether or not you agree with the saying and why. For Topic B, list the reasons why you believe space exploration is or is not important.

Step 4—Writing Your First Draft

Use your notes from prewriting to help you write your first draft. Focus on content.

Step 5—Sharing Your Draft

Working with a classmate, read each other's draft. Give feedback to each other using this format:

A. Reading for Content

1. What do you like most about this paper?
2. What would you still like to know more about?
3. What suggestions do you have for the writer?

B. Checking for Errors in Subject-Verb Agreement

1. Circle any errors in subject-verb agreement you notice on your classmate's draft.
2. Discuss how to correct them.

Step 6—Revising Your Writing

Using your classmate's suggestions as well as your own ideas for revising, write your second draft. Focus on content and sentence-level accuracy. In particular, check whether your subject-verb agreement is accurate.

Step 7—Proofreading Your Final Draft

Read your final draft once again, paying particular attention to subject-verb agreement. Make any necessary changes.

Postwriting Activity

Step 1—When your paper is returned, check to see if your instructor has marked any errors in subject-verb agreement.

Step 2—If so, review the material in *Part II* of this unit.

Step 3—Correct each error in subject-verb agreement by rewriting the sentence that contains the error. If you are unsure of the correction, ask a classmate or your instructor for help.

■ PART V: Applying What You Have Learned to Other Writing Assignments

In Part V, you will

- *look for and correct subject-verb agreement errors in any other writing assignments you have done*

If you are in a composition class or another class in which you do writing, take your last returned writing assignment and do the following:

1. Check whether your instructor has marked any errors in subject-verb agreement on your paper. If so, try to correct them using the material you have learned in this unit as a guide.

2. If your instructor has not marked any errors in subject-verb agreement, take one paragraph and underline each verb and its subject. Try to determine whether subject-verb agreement is correct. If you are not sure, ask a classmate or your instructor to help you.

3. When you do writing assignments in the future, be sure to check for errors in subject-verb agreement.

UNIT 11: ARTICLE*

*art = grading symbol for article errors

■ PART I: What You Need to Know About Article Errors

> **In Part I,** *you will answer the following questions:*
> * *What is an article error?*
> * *Why is it important to avoid article errors in writing?*
> * *What are some strategies for mastering articles?*

Definition of the Error

An article error (**art**) is one in which the article has been used incorrectly. The articles, which belong to the group of modifiers called determiners, are *a(n)*, Ø (the zero article), and *the*. The articles *a* and Ø are indefinite and *the* is a definite article. Before vowel sounds, *an* is used instead of *a*. (In this unit, *a* automatically includes *an*.)

Importance of Mastering Article Use in Writing

Errors in article use are local (less serious) errors and usually do not greatly affect how well the reader can understand what you have written. However, frequent article errors are distracting and can lead the reader to focus on article errors rather than on content. Although in spoken English article errors may not be very noticeable, in formal written English, article errors cannot be ignored.

Suggestions for Mastering Article Use

The rules governing **all** the uses of the article are complex; however, the rules given in this unit will help you use the article correctly in most cases. You can then look up additional rules as you need them in an advanced ESL grammar book. If your native language does not contain articles, you must learn the rules for articles. However, even if your native language uses articles, you will need to become aware of any differences in their use in English.

Memorizing the use of the article with words or phases that you often use will also help you master the article. A particularly good strategy is to memorize phrases and terminology in your major and in classes you are taking.

Because the article is not stressed in spoken English, listening will not help you very much in learning how to use articles. Therefore, to learn how to use articles correctly, you should practice using them in writing and you should observe their use in your reading. What is most important to remember is that while mastering the article is very difficult, just improving the percentage of articles you use correctly will make your writing easier to read.

TEST YOUR UNDERSTANDING OF ARTICLES

After you have read *Part I*, write answers to the following questions. Share your answers with another student.

1. What is an article? Explain in your own words.
2. How serious are article errors in writing? Explain your answer.
3. Does your native language have articles? If so, are they used in the same way as in English or are they used differently in your language?
4. Do you think you use articles correctly? If not, discuss two strategies that you could adopt to improve your ability to use articles correctly.

■ PART II: Common Problems, Rules, and Self-help Strategies

In Part II, you will

- *study four problems ESL writers commonly have with articles*
- *learn selected grammar rules for controlling articles*

This section presents four problems ESL writers commonly have with articles. First, study each problem and the examples that illustrate it. Then mark the problems you think you have when you write in English. Remember that if you become aware of the type of article errors you most often make, you will increase your chances of avoiding these errors in your writing.

Selected grammar rules that explain how to use *a*, Ø, and *the* follow the problems.[1]

---

1. The material in this section is based in part on the binary system for teaching articles developed by Peter Master and reported in "Teaching the English Articles as a Binary System," *TESOL Quarterly*, vol. 24, no. 3, Autumn, 1990.

PROBLEM 1. The zero article (Ø) has been used when *a* or *the* is needed.

Incorrect: Yesterday, I finally went to pay my overdue fine at‸library.

Correct: Yesterday, I finally went to pay my overdue fine at <u>the</u> library.

Incorrect: She bought‸book and‸ballpoint pen as‸birthday gift.

Correct: She bought <u>a</u> book and <u>a</u> ballpoint pen as <u>a</u> birthday gift.

Incorrect: All of‸textbooks for this class have been sold.

Correct: All of <u>the</u> textbooks for this class have been sold.

PROBLEM 2. The article *a* has been used where Ø is needed.

Incorrect: A good friend gives <u>an</u> advice when asked.

Correct: A good friend gives advice when asked.

Incorrect: My uncle has <u>an</u> obvious reasons for his decision.

Correct: My uncle has obvious reasons for his decision.

PROBLEM 3. The article *a* has been used for *the* or vice versa.

Incorrect: My cousin lived <u>the</u> productive life as a pharmacist.

Correct: My cousin lived <u>a</u> productive life as a pharmacist.

Incorrect: My lab partner has <u>a</u> books you wanted him to find.

Correct: My lab partner has <u>the</u> books you wanted him to find.

PROBLEM 4. The articles *a*, Ø, or *the* have been used instead of another determiner.

Note: Articles are part of the whole system of determiners, which includes possessive pronouns (for example: *my, your*), demonstrative adjectives (*this, these; that, those*), and quantifiers (for example: *some, any* or *every*).

Incorrect: Whenever I go to the library, I remember that I need <u>the</u> library card.

Correct: Whenever I go to the library, I remember that I need <u>my</u> library card. (*I need a library card* would also be correct but would not show possession.)

Incorrect: Restaurant employees need to wash <u>the</u> hands frequently.

Correct: Restaurant employees need to wash <u>their</u> hands frequently.

Incorrect: She wants <u>a</u> meat for dinner.

Correct: She wants <u>some</u> meat for dinner. (The emphasis is on the amount.)

Correct: She wants meat for dinner. (The emphasis is not on the amount but on what she wants to eat for dinner.)

Rules for Identifying Versus Not Identifying a Common Noun

In this section, you will learn selected rules for using articles with common nouns. Every time you use a common noun or noun phrase (the noun plus its modifiers) in English, you must decide between *a*, Ø, or *the*. Articles are used to identify or not identify a noun as specified below.

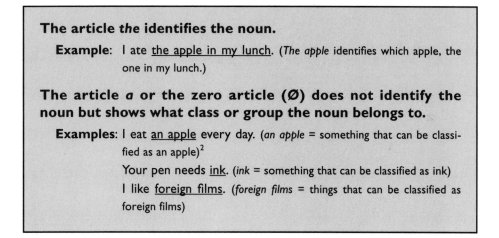

The article *the* identifies the noun.

> **Example**: I ate <u>the apple in my lunch</u>. (*The apple* identifies which apple, the one in my lunch.)

The article *a* or the zero article (Ø) does not identify the noun but shows what class or group the noun belongs to.

> **Examples**: I eat <u>an apple</u> every day. (*an apple* = something that can be classified as an apple)[2]
>
> Your pen needs <u>ink</u>. (*ink* = something that can be classified as ink)
>
> I like <u>foreign films</u>. (*foreign films* = things that can be classified as foreign films)

1. When you are not identifying a common noun, use *a* or Ø.

   You will decide to use *a* or Ø depending upon whether the noun is countable or uncountable. Countable nouns (like *textbook*, *test*, or *assignment*) can be counted and made plural, but uncountable nouns (like *writing*, *homework*, and *intelligence*) cannot be counted and do not have a plural form. Most ESL dictionaries indicate if a noun is countable or uncountable. Some nouns (like *paper* or *change*) can be either countable or uncountable depending on their meaning.

   a. If the noun is a singular countable noun, use *a*.

Incorrect:	Last week I bought $\overset{art}{\wedge}$chemistry textbook at Aggie Books.
Correct:	Last week I bought <u>a</u> chemistry textbook at Aggie Books.
	(The chemistry textbook is one of many chemistry texts the bookstore has; the writer has not identified the particular book.)

---

2. The wording "something that can be classified as . . . " comes from Peter Master's work on the binary schema of articles.

Incorrect: When students are taking *art* the composition class, they often complain about the time they must spend working on their essays.

Correct: When students are taking a composition class, they often complain about the time they must spend working on their essays. (The writer has not identified a specific class but is talking about any composition class.)

b. If the noun is uncountable or if it is plural, use Ø.

Note: The determiner *some* can be used with uncountable and plural nouns but only when an amount can be indicated.

Incorrect: Many people drink *art* the bottled water since they prefer its taste.

Correct: Many people drink bottled water since they prefer its taste. (Water is uncountable.)

Incorrect: *art* The playing badminton is my favorite activity.

Correct: Playing badminton is my favorite activity.
(Gerunds and gerund phrases [the gerund with its object and modifiers] are uncountable.)

Incorrect: Before I go to class, I had better buy *art* a ruled notebook paper.

Correct: Before I go to class, I had better buy ruled notebook paper. (Paper is uncountable and no amount is specified.)

Correct: Before I go to class, I had better buy some ruled notebook paper. (Paper is uncountable and a nonspecific amount is indicated.)

Incorrect: *art* The rubber-soled shoes are to be worn at all times on the gymnasium floor.

Correct: Rubber-soled shoes are to be worn at all times on the gymnasium floor. (The writer means rubber-soled shoes of any kind.)

Incorrect: *art* The blue books are to be used during the final exam.

Correct: Blue books are to be used during the final exam.
(The writer has not identified any specific blue books.)

2. When you are identifying a common noun, use *the*.

a. After you have used a noun with *a*, use *the* when you use the noun again.

Incorrect: I found a used car that I liked yesterday and bought it. I now have to buy insurance for *art* a car.

Correct: I found a used car that I liked yesterday and bought it. I now have to buy insurance for the car. (*The* car means specifically the car that has already been mentioned.)

b. **When the following occur, use *the*. The noun can be singular or plural, countable or uncountable.**

- The noun is identified by a ranking adjective that identifies it as one of a kind:

  Correct: <u>The best</u> ice cream is sold at that shop. (a superlative)

  Correct: In <u>the next</u> chapter, we will examine verb tense. (sequential)

  Correct: She is <u>the only</u> student with whom I will study. (unique)

- The noun is identifiable to the reader and the writer through shared knowledge.

  Correct: <u>The sun</u> is going to rise at 5:43 A.M. tomorrow. (Both reader and writer know which sun.)

  Correct: My roommate left her backpack in <u>the computer room</u>. (Both reader and writer know which room it is.)

  Correct: Some of <u>the students</u> will need to take a make-up test. (Both reader and writer know who the students are).

- The noun phrase is identified by the modification that follows it.

  Correct: Last week I finally read <u>the article about thunderstorms that Professor Johns recommended to us</u>. (The article has been identified as the one about thunderstorms and the one that was recommended.)

  Correct: Most of the <u>textbooks for this class</u> have been sold. (The textbooks have been identified as the ones for a certain class.)

  Correct: <u>The laughter of the children</u> made my grandfather happy. (The noun has been identified by an *of* phrase.)

  Correct: <u>The laughing of his grandchildren</u> made my grandfather happy. (Note that when a gerund or gerund phrase is modified, it is identified and thus uses *the*. The gerund phrase *playing badminton* is not identified but if its direct object becomes an *of* phrase modifying the gerund, the gerund is then identified as in *the playing of badminton*.)

Rules for Using Articles with Proper Nouns

In academic and professional writing, you will often need to use the names of people and places. When you are naming a particular person or place, you will use a proper noun, which is always capitalized. Because the rules for using articles with proper nouns have many exceptions, it is best to learn only a few general rules and to memorize article use for those proper nouns you frequently employ. You can also check article use for individual cases in an advanced ESL grammar book or an ESL dictionary for advanced language learners, or you can simply ask a native speaker what is correct.

For names of people, use the following guidelines:

- With singular names of people, Ø is usually used.

  Examples: Have you read *The Tale of Two Cities* by <u>Charles Dickens</u>?

  <u>Miriam</u> has just finished a French quiz.

  <u>Dr. Hendrickson</u> will be a guest lecturer in my history class on Tuesday.

- With plural family names, *the* is usually used.

  Example: Next week <u>the Campbells</u> will talk about their life as pioneers in Montana.

For names of places, use the following guidelines:

- States, cities, streets, and universities usually use Ø unless the name is introduced by a capitalized common noun (such as *City* or *University*) and *of*.

  Examples: Last night, I telephoned my brother who attends <u>Stanford University</u> in <u>Palo Alto</u>, <u>California</u>.

  The bank is located on <u>State Street</u>.

  My sister works as a public defender for <u>The City of New York</u>.

  <u>The University of Arizona</u> is on the semester system.

- Oceans, rivers, mountain ranges, and public buildings usually use *the*.

  Examples: <u>The Pacific Ocean</u> keeps San Francisco cool.

  <u>The Mississippi River</u> starts in Minnesota and ends in Louisiana.

  <u>The Rocky Mountains</u> have good snow for skiing.

  <u>The Metropolitan Museum of Art</u> is on Fifth Avenue.

Rules for Using Articles with Set Expressions

Certain set (or common) expressions use *the* or Ø. To make sure that you are using the correct article, either look up the expression in an ESL dictionary or ask a native speaker what is correct. It is also a good idea to memorize set expressions that you use frequently.

The following brief list will help you become aware of article use in set expressions:

with Ø article	with <u>the</u>
by train, by plane, by car	on <u>the</u> other hand
to church, to school	<u>the</u> Establishment
at seven o'clock	in <u>the</u> morning
on vacation	in <u>the</u> evening
in class	in <u>the</u> afternoon
for example	to get <u>the</u> gist of
at home, at school	to get <u>the</u> point
at night	to play <u>the</u> part
after breakfast	

■ PART III: Exercises

In Part III, you will practice
- *recognizing and correcting article errors in individual sentences*
- *explaining why a, Ø, or the is used in a paragraph*
- *recognizing and correcting article errors in a paragraph*
- *explaining why a, Ø, or the is used in a reading selection*

EXERCISE I   (Do this exercise on your own. Then check your answers with a classmate.)

Directions: Test your ability to identify and correct article errors in the following sentences. First, decide if a sentence is correct (C) or if it contains any article errors (I). Then correct each article error. Some sentences may have more than one article error, and some errors can be corrected in more than one way.

> **Examples:** __I__ Cheryl forgot to turn in ∧*the* assignment for her math class.
>
> __C__ Will you stop at the grocery store on your way home?

_____1. At the end of each quarter, a final exams are held.

_____2. Most of students in Chemistry 1 have to study very hard.

_____3. She went to the bookstore and bought pencils, a textbook, and glue.

_____4. If students ride their bikes to school, they need to make sure that brakes on their bicycles are working.

_____5. At the night, all patrons must wear the shirts and ties in this restaurant.

_____6. One of best recent inventions has been the computer.

_____7. If I have problems with my car, I take bus to work.

_____8. Be sure that you study night before exam.

_____9. Instant noodles are quick and easy to prepare.

_____10. When there is full moon, I like to walk down the Beach Avenue.

_____11. In California, the water is a precious commodity when there is a drought.

_____12. Although I like to write down my thoughts, I never have enough time to write in the journal.

EXERCISE 2 (Do this exercise with a classmate).

Directions: In the following paragraph, adapted from writing by a student, the articles have been used correctly. Examine the underlined nouns and noun phrases and explain why *a*, Ø or *the* was used.

uncountable, not identified
My parents taught me to love <u>learning</u> when I was still very young.

Every evening after <u>dinner</u>, my father would teach me <u>simple math</u> and

my mother would teach me how to write and read <u>Chinese characters</u>. At

the age of five, I already knew a number of Chinese characters and was able to do addition, <u>subtraction</u>, and <u>simple multiplication problems</u>. It wasn't that I was <u>a genius</u> or even a precocious child; it was <u>the simple fact</u> that my parents encouraged me to learn by praising me whenever I gave them <u>the correct answer</u> to their questions. Their praise made me feel that I was smart and could learn. What also helped me learn was that I had <u>few distractions</u>. I did not grow up with <u>a television</u>, a radio, or <u>video games</u> as children do now, for it was not common in <u>China</u> at that time to have a television or a radio at home. Therefore, our usual source of entertainment after dinner was <u>playing games</u>, <u>reading</u>, and learning. When I began school, I never had to depend on <u>the teacher</u> to motivate me to learn because I had already developed a love of learning. I also entered <u>school</u> with the attitude that I could learn because my parents' early teaching and <u>the learning</u> that had taken place in my house had helped me develop not only <u>confidence</u> in my abilities but also <u>a sense</u> that learning was enjoyable.

Respond to What You Have Read

Answer each question with a short written response. Check your answers carefully for article use and then share them with a classmate.

1. Was your early experience with learning similar to or different from the writer's? Explain.
2. Do you think children should start learning at an early age or do you think that they should have more time to play?

EXERCISE 3   (Do this exercise with a classmate.)

Directions: The following paragraph, which was written by a student, has some articles left out. Test your mastery of articles by supplying the correct articles where needed. The first one has been done for you.

My attitude toward English is negatively affecting my writing. I think the problem is that as ^*a* mathematics major, I love to spend my time doing as much math as possible. Often my math homework and my other classes, which also relate to my major, occupy most of my time. As a result, I devote rest of my time and energy, which is not much, to writing essays for my English class. However, I usually have trouble getting started. I waste my time eating, listening to music, or even looking in the mirror instead of trying to work on my paper. Furthermore, I always have negative feeling toward writing. Even before writing paper, I assume that my paper will not turn out well. Because of this negative attitude, my grade in English is suffering.

EXERCISE 4   (Do this exercise on your own. Then check your answers with a classmate.)

Directions: Choose a short article in a newspaper or a magazine and read it. Then underline all the nouns or noun phrases in two paragraphs and explain why the author used *a*, Ø, or *the*.

■ PART IV: Writing Activity

In Part IV, you will

- *plan and write a response to a selected topic*
- *share your writing with a classmate*
- *edit your writing for content and sentence-level accuracy*

Step 1—Choosing a Writing Topic

Select one or both of the following:

Topic A: A friend has never seen where you live. Write a letter to your friend in which you describe your room or your apartment. If you live in a house, describe only your room. In your letter, be sure to tell your friend how comfortable you are living in this place or room.

Topic B: How, in your opinion, can reading help ESL students improve their English skills?

Step 2—Gathering Information

With a classmate or in a small group, discuss possible places you consider your true home or discuss ways in which reading can help ESL students improve their English.

Step 3—Prewriting

Working by yourself, list two or three reasons why you have chosen this place as your true home or list two or three ways in which reading can help ESL students improve their English. Under each reason or way, jot down examples that illustrate your point.

Step 4—Writing Your First Draft

Use your list from prewriting to help you write your first draft. Focus on content.

Step 5—Sharing Your Draft

Working with a classmate, read each other's draft. Give feedback to each other by completing the following:

A. Reading for Content

1. What did you like most about this piece of writing?
2. What would you still like to know more about?
3. What suggestions do you have for the writer?

B. Checking for Article Errors

1. Circle any article errors you notice on your classmate's draft.
2. Discuss how to correct them.

Step 6—Revising Your Writing

Using your classmate's suggestions as well as your own ideas for revising, write your second draft. Focus on content and sentence-level accuracy. In particular, check your use of articles and correct any errors with articles. You might, for instance, underline all the nouns in two paragraphs and check whether or not you have used *a*, Ø, and *the* correctly. If you are unsure whether a noun is countable, check the noun in an ESL dictionary and then apply the rules you have learned in this unit. For article use with set expressions, check an ESL dictionary. For article use with proper nouns, check under articles in an ESL grammar book.

Step 7—Proofreading Your Final Draft

Read your final draft once again, looking in particular at your use of articles. Make any necessary changes.

Postwriting Activity

Step 1—When your response is returned, check to see if your instructor has marked any errors in article use.

Step 2—If so, review the material in *Part II* of this unit.

Step 3—Correct each article error by rewriting the sentence that contains the error. If you are unsure of the answer, ask your instructor for help.

■ PART V: Applying What You Have Learned to Other Writing Assignments

In Part V, you will

• *look for and correct article errors in any other writing assignments you have done*

If you are in a composition class or another class in which you do writing, take your last returned paper and follow these directions:

1. Check whether your instructor has marked any article errors on your paper. If so, try to correct them, using the material you have learned in this unit as a guide.

2. If your instructor has not marked any article errors on your paper, take one paragraph and underline each noun or noun phrase. Try to determine whether the article use is correct. If you are not sure, ask a classmate or your instructor to help you.

3. When you do writing assignments in the future, be sure to check for article errors.

UNIT 12: NUMBER*

*num = grading symbol for number errors

■ PART I: What You Need to Know About Number Errors

> **In Part I, you will answer the following questions:**
> - *What is a number error?*
> - *Why is it important to avoid number errors in writing?*
> - *What are some strategies for mastering number?*

Definition of the Error

A number error (**num**) is one in which the singular form of a noun has been used instead of the plural or vice versa. For example, in the sentence *I have two sister,* there is a number error because *sister* should be *sisters*. Likewise, in the sentence *He gave me some informations,* there is also a number error because *informations* should be *information*.

Importance of Mastering Number in Writing

Number errors are local errors and usually do not affect the meaning of a sentence, but frequent errors in number can distract the reader's attention from the content of a piece of writing. While mistakes in singular and plural are sometimes tolerated in speaking, readers expect to see the correct use of number in written academic English.

Suggestions for Mastering Number

If your native language does not make nouns plural, you must train yourself to use the singular and plural correctly in English. Even if your native language indicates number much as English does, you must still become aware of differences between your language and English in the use of singulars and plurals.

Because the plural *s* is not stressed in spoken English and often is difficult to hear, plural nouns may sound singular to you. For example, when an instructor says, "I want you to read three chapters for tomorrow," the first syllable, *chap*, will be said louder and longer than *ters* and the *s* will be hard to hear. Thus, you cannot necessarily rely on your ear to help you learn how to use the singular and plural. However, by paying careful attention to singulars and plurals of nouns while you are reading and by becoming aware of the rules for number (which you will read about in this unit), you can reduce many of your number errors in writing.

The general rule is that countable nouns (like *textbook*, *test*, or *assignment*) can be made plural by adding *-s* or *-es* but that uncountable nouns (like *writing*, *homework*, and *stress*) cannot.[1] If you are unsure whether a noun is countable or not, look up the word in an ESL dictionary. However, when you are writing, it is wise to simply mark nouns that you need to check for number. In that way, you can revise for number later and not disrupt your focus on content while searching for a noun in the dictionary.

Another wise step is to memorize certain singular and plural forms of nouns that you use often in your classes or in your field of study. As a first step, always put the ending *-s* on *the United States* and do not add an *-s* to *homework*!

TEST YOUR UNDERSTANDING OF NUMBER

After you have read *Part I*, write answers to the following questions. Share your answers with another student.

1. What is a number error? Explain in your own words.
2. Are number errors global or local? Explain your answer.
3. Why should ESL writers master number? Give two reasons.
4. What three strategies can ESL writers use to avoid making number errors?

■ PART II: Common Problems, Rules, and Self-help Strategies

In Part II, you will

- *study seven common problems ESL writers have with number*
- *learn selected rules and strategies for mastering number in writing*

This section presents seven problems that ESL writers commonly have with number. First, study each problem and the examples that illustrate it. Then

---

1. Nouns can be classified into those that are countable versus those that are uncountable (often also called mass or noncountable nouns). Countable nouns have singulars and plurals (*book, books),* and individual members of a group can be counted (*one book, two books, three books*). Uncountable nouns have only one form (*money, air, happiness*) and cannot be counted. We **cannot** say *one money, one air,* or *one happiness.* Note that uncountable nouns take a singular verb (*The air is fresh*).

mark the problems you think you have when you write in English. Remember that if you become aware of the type of number errors you most often make, you will increase your chances of avoiding these errors in your writing.

PROBLEM 1. A countable noun is singular when it should be plural.

Incorrect: The *num* <u>student</u> in the class were taking <u>note</u>.
Correct: The <u>students</u> in the class were taking <u>notes</u>.
Incorrect: I solved all but two *num* <u>problem</u> on my calculus test.
Correct: I solved all but two <u>problems</u> on my calculus test.

Self-help Strategy: Look at the countable noun and ask yourself whether you are dealing with just one or more than one. Countable nouns are made plural by adding *s* or *es*.

PROBLEM 2. An uncountable noun has been made plural.

Incorrect: I need to do my *num* <u>homeworks</u>.
Correct: I need to do my <u>homework</u>.
Incorrect: Water consists of two parts <u>hydrogens</u> *num* and one part <u>oxygens</u>.
Correct: Water consists of two parts <u>hydrogen</u> and one part <u>oxygen</u>.

Self-help Strategy: Look at the noun and ask yourself whether it is countable or uncountable. Remember that countable nouns can be made plural, but uncountable nouns do not become plural; that is, they do not add *-s* or *-es*. If you are unsure, look the noun up in a dictionary for non-native English speakers to see if it is countable or uncountable.

PROBLEM 3. A noun and its demonstrative adjective do not agree in number.

Incorrect: <u>These *num* book</u> are for the other class, not yours.
Correct: <u>These books</u> are for the other class, not yours.
Correct: <u>This book</u> is for the other class, not yours.

Rule: Demonstrative adjectives agree in number with the noun they modify. The demonstrative adjectives are: *this, that* = singular
these, those = plural

PROBLEM 4. A noun or adjective modifying a noun has been made plural.

Incorrect: The campus is made up of <u>reds *num* bricks</u> buildings.
Correct: The campus is made up of <u>red brick</u> buildings.

Incorrect: Next week we have to write a <u>five-hundreds-words</u> *num* essay.

Correct: Next week we have to write a <u>five-hundred-word</u> essay.

Rule: Adjectives can never be made plural in English. Nouns used as adjectives are also singular.

Examples: <u>one</u> <u>white</u> house, <u>two</u> <u>white</u> houses
                <u>one</u> <u>chocolate</u> bar, <u>two</u> <u>chocolate</u> bars

Self-help Strategy: If your native language makes adjectives plural to agree with the noun, be especially careful to avoid this error in English.

PROBLEM 5. An idiomatic expression has been incorrectly made singular or plural.

Incorrect: To make a good decision, you need to weigh the <u>pro and con</u>. *num*

Correct: To make a good decision, you need to weigh the <u>pros and cons</u>.

Incorrect: Robert wears the same old shirt <u>days after days</u>. *num*

Correct: Robert wears the same old shirt <u>day after day</u>.

Self-help Strategy: Idiomatic expressions often have to be memorized. If you are unsure, look up the expression in a dictionary for nonnative English speakers. Such a dictionary often includes idiomatic expressions.

PROBLEM 6. A countable noun following an *of* phrase has not been made plural or an uncountable noun following an *of* phrase has been made plural. (Some *of* phrases are *one of the, most of the, any of the, half of the,* or *some of the.*)

Incorrect: One of the oldest <u>building</u> on campus is North Hall. *num*

Correct: One of the oldest <u>buildings</u> on campus is North Hall.

Incorrect: Some of the <u>milks</u> has gone sour. *num*

Correct: Some of the <u>milk</u> has gone sour.
             (Milk is not countable.)

Rule: A countable noun after these phrases is always plural. An uncountable noun after these phrases is always singular.

Self-help Strategy: Make it a habit to revise your work carefully to see if you have used the singular or plural of the noun correctly after an *of* phrase.

PROBLEM 7. A countable noun that has an irregular plural has been incorrectly formed.

Incorrect: Five <u>womans</u> signed up for the auto mechanics class. *num*

Correct: Five <u>women</u> signed up for the auto mechanics class.

num

Incorrect: Paul is doing research on <u>childs</u> and their eating habits.

Correct: Paul is doing research on <u>children</u> and their eating habits.

Self-help Strategy: Be aware that some nouns in English have an irregular plural. Common examples are *tooth*, *teeth*; *fish*, *fish*; *thesis*, *theses*.

■ PART III: Exercises

In Part III, you will practice

- *recognizing and correcting number errors in individual sentences*
- *recognizing and correcting number errors in a paragraph*
- *deciding the correct form (singular or plural) of nouns in a paragraph*

EXERCISE I (Do this exercise on your own. Then check your answers with a classmate.)

Directions: Using the material you have just studied as a guide, underline and then correct any errors with number in the following sentences.

Example: Please don't forget to buy some <u>banana</u>ˢ on your way home.

1. When I read, I mark unfamiliar vocabularies, which I later look up in a dictionary.

2. This boys needs to sign up for the camping trip.

3. One of the best way to practice your English is to join a conversation club.

4. Many cultures teach respect for the elderlies.

5. I had three piece of candies and some cake at the party.

6. My writing needs improvements, so I am going to work with a tutor.

7. My friends are renting a hundreds-year-old house.

8. The professor is hiring students to analyze the datas she collected.

9. You need to follow the laboratory manual steps by steps to make your experiment come out right.

10. I had almost given up finding my watch when it suddenly caught my eyes from under a piece of paper.

11. My aunt has five childs: two sons and three daughter.

12. My roommate has excellent computers skills.

EXERCISE 2   (Do this exercise on your own. Then check your answers with a classmate.)

Directions: In the following paragraph, which was written by a student, selected nouns and adjectives have been underlined. Decide whether you need to make the word plural or leave it singular. Make any corrections by adding the appropriate ending or crossing out the word and rewriting it above.

During the fall quarter, I was overwhelmed with many <u>assignment</u>. The most unexpected one was writing. Even though I knew that education <u>class</u> required <u>writing</u>, the professors I had were especially fond of <u>essay</u> writing. Both of my education <u>class</u> required a total of eight <u>paper</u>, each of which were four to six <u>page</u> long; in addition, the final papers in both classes were twenty-page <u>research</u> papers. Furthermore, both of my biochemistry <u>class</u> required a total of eight lab write-ups and three essays. In sum, I had to write more than twenty papers last quarter, and <u>that</u> papers were a nightmare for me. Previously, I thought that only English classes would require a lot of writing which is not one of my favorite <u>activity</u>. Nevertheless, last semester was the only time during my four years in college that I had to write so much. Thus, I lost much of my <u>fear</u> of writing; however, I still hate <u>revision</u> because it is very time-consuming <u>work</u>.

EXERCISE 3 (Do this exercise with a classmate.)

Directions: In the following paragraph, some errors in number occur. Do this exercise by following these steps:

1. Underline each noun and any adjectives that modify the noun.
2. Using *Part II* as a guide, determine where errors in number occur in the paragraph.
3. If you are unsure whether a noun can take the plural or not, check a dictionary for nonnative English speakers to see if the noun is countable or uncountable.
4. Correct any number errors by writing the correct form above the noun or adjective. Make the verb agree with the corrected noun as necessary.

Catalog shopping has become very popular in the United State.[s] According to a recent newspaper article, catalog sales have been growing at the rate of 15 percent annually, twice the growth rate of retail store sales. With the advents of 800 number and fax machines, catalog shopping has indeed become fast and convenient. You can telephone in your order, speak to the salesperson at the other end, and usually find out if what you want is in stock, thus avoiding the tedious works of filling out an order form. Or, if you prefer a written record, you can use the order form provided in the catalog and fax it to the catalog company. These days, it is possible to buy everything from a simple white blouse to a whole set of garden furnitures without ever setting foot in a store. Most people also like the option of express mail that catalogs companies offer; customers can send an order one day and the item will arrive at their house a day or two after. People also find that if they purchase clothings from the same catalog companies, they can avoid much frustrations, for they can almost always gauge the right size. Also, catalogs help by showing a picture of the range of colors. However, what the catalogs do not mention is that while you can return your purchase, it is time-consuming to repack and send it. Thus, if you get what you wanted, you have saved time. However, if you are disappointed, you will have to devote time to repackaging and returning the item. If you are too busy or lazy to do so and thus keep the unwanted item, you will lose money. However, a wonderful alternatives is the catalog store. You can see what you want in the catalog and then go to the catalog store and buy it. Then you have the best of both world.

EXERCISE 4 (Do this exercise on your own.)

Directions: Choose and read a short article in a newspaper or a magazine. Then underline ten nouns in the article. Using the information you have learned in this unit, decide why the noun is singular or plural. If you are unsure why a noun is in the singular, check in an ESL dictionary to determine if it is an uncountable noun and, therefore, cannot be made plural.

EXERCISE 5 (Do this exercise on your own.)

Directions: List ten nouns that you commonly use in your major field or in a field that interests you. Then write two sentences for each word—one in which you use the word in the singular and the other in which you use it in the plural, if it is possible to make the noun plural. If necessary, use an ESL dictionary to check whether the noun is countable or uncountable.

■ PART IV: Writing Activity

In Part IV, you will
- *plan and write a response to a selected topic*
- *share your writing with a classmate*
- *edit your writing for content and sentence-level accuracy*

Step 1—Choosing a Writing Topic

Select one or more of the following:

Topic A: Discuss your favorite ways to relieve stress. Explain how they are beneficial to you.

Topic B: Stress has been named as a contributing factor to a host of health-related problems. Discuss what some causes of stress are and how the resulting stress affects people's emotional and physical well-being. In your conclusion, be sure to suggest some remedies for stress.

Step 2—Gathering Information

Work with a classmate or in a small group. For Topic A, discuss ways you relax from the stress of schoolwork or your job. In addition, talk about how these ways to combat stress are beneficial to you both mentally and physically. For Topic B, discuss what some of the causes of stress are and how the resulting stress affects people's emotional and physical well-being.

Step 3—Prewriting

Work by yourself. For Topic A, list two or three ways you relax from stress. Under each way, jot down notes to illustrate how each way helps you relieve stress. Then, in one sentence, summarize how your ways to relieve stress benefit you overall. For Topic B, list three sources of stress. Under each source you have identified, jot down notes to illustrate how this stress affects people's emotional and physical health. Try to think of examples from your own experience to illustrate your points.

Step 4—Writing Your First Draft

Using what you have done in your prewriting, write your first draft. Focus on content.

Step 5—Sharing Your Draft

Working with a classmate, read each other's draft. Give feedback to each other by completing the following:

A. Reading for Content

1. What did you like most about this piece of writing?
2. What would you still like to know more about?
3. What suggestions do you have for the writer?

B. Checking for Number Errors

1. Circle any number errors you notice on your classmate's draft.
2. Discuss how to correct them.

Step 6—Revising Your Writing

Using your classmate's suggestions as well as your own ideas for revising, write your second draft, focusing on content and sentence-level accuracy. Pay special attention to how you have used singulars and plurals and correct any errors you have made with number.

Step 7—Proofreading Your Final Draft

Read your final draft once again, looking in particular at your use of singulars and plurals. Make any necessary changes.

Postwriting Activity

Step 1—When your response is returned, check to see if your instructor has marked any errors in number.

Step 2—If so, review the material in *Part II* of this unit.

Step 3—Correct each number error by rewriting the sentence that contains the error. If you are unsure of the answer, ask your instructor for help.

■ PART V: Applying What You Have Learned to Other Writing Assignments

In Part V, you will

• *look for and correct number errors in any other writing assignments you have done*

If you are in a composition class or another class in which you do writing, take your last returned paper and follow these directions:

1. Check whether your instructor has marked any number errors on your paper. If so, try to correct them, using what you have learned in this unit.

2. If your instructor has not marked any number errors on your paper, take one paragraph and underline each noun. Try to determine whether the nouns are correct in number. If you are not sure, ask a classmate or your instructor to help you.

3. When you do writing assignments in the future, be sure to check for number errors.

UNIT 13: WORD CHOICE*

*wc = grading symbol for word-choice errors

209

■ PART I: What You Need to Know About Errors in Word Choice

> ### In Part I, you will answer the following questions:
> - What is an error in word choice?
> - Why is it important to avoid word-choice errors in writing?
> - What are some strategies for mastering word choice?

Definition of the Error

A word-choice error (**wc**) is one in which the wrong word has been used in a sentence. For example, in the sentence *Even though she spoke very little English when she first arrived in the United States, my mother did not <u>abundant</u> her dream of being a bookkeeper,* the word *abundant* should be *abandon.*

Word-choice errors, although frequently local (less serious) and affecting only part of a sentence, can become global (more serious) when they affect a reader's ability to understand a significant portion of a text.

Importance of Mastering Word Choice in Writing

To convey exact meaning, the writer must master word choice. When a writer uses a word incorrectly, the reader must then either guess the meaning or skip the word altogether. Thus, the reader, instead of the writer, is supplying meaning which may or may not be correct. Such work tires the reader and can cause him or her to lose interest in a piece of writing.

Suggestions for Mastering Word Choice

Word choice is governed not by rules but by usage. You may find it very helpful to use an ESL dictionary that shows, for example, how a word is used in a sentence or indicates which preposition goes with a word. If you also use a thesaurus, you need to choose words carefully from it, making sure that each word you have selected fits in your sentence. It is particularly valuable to double-check the word in an ESL dictionary that illustrates the word in a sample sentence. Another useful reference tool is a lexicon in which words are organized by topics.

It is also valuable to memorize how certain words are used, particularly words that you use frequently in your major or fields of interest. Most importantly, you should avoid, as much as possible, translating from your language into English since direct translation often results in word-choice problems.

Because there are no rules for word choice, you will sometimes need to ask a native speaker if you have used a word correctly.

TEST YOUR UNDERSTANDING OF WORD CHOICE

After you have read *Part I*, write answers to the following questions. Share your answers with another student.

1. What is an error in word choice? Explain in your own words.
2. Why can word-choice errors be either local (less serious) or global (more serious)?
3. Why does the reader have difficulty when the wrong word is used?
4. How can you improve your ability to choose words correctly?

■ PART II: Common Problems, Rules, and Self-help Strategies

In Part II, you will

* *study five problems ESL writers commonly have with word choice*
* *learn rules and self-help strategies for controlling word choice*

This section presents five problems ESL writers commonly have with word choice. First, study each problem and the examples that illustrate it. Then mark the problems you think you have when you write in English. Remember that if you become aware of the type of word-choice errors you most often make, you will increase your chances of avoiding these errors in your writing.

PROBLEM 1. A wrong word has been used in a sentence.

Note: Prepositions are treated in Problem 2, which follows. Conjunctions are treated separately in *Unit 7*.

Incorrect: The essay we just read is an exception from a longer work.

Correct: The essay we just read is an excerpt from a longer work.

Incorrect: There will be a 40 percent increase in <u>intuition</u>^{*wc*} fees this year.

Correct: There will be a 40 percent increase in <u>tuition</u> fees this year.

Incorrect: My inability to communicate with others in English always <u>bounds</u>^{*wc*} our friendship at a superficial level.

Correct: My inability to communicate with others in English always <u>keeps</u> our friendship at a superficial level.

Self-help Strategy: If you are unsure about the word you have chosen, you will want to look it up in an ESL dictionary, preferably one that gives example sentences showing how the word is used.

PROBLEM 2. A wrong preposition has been used.

Note: Some instructors may simply mark this error as *prep*.

Incorrect: My brother lives <u>in</u>^{*wc*} Anderson Street.

Correct: My brother lives <u>on</u> Anderson Street.

Incorrect: My math teacher always praised me when I gave the correct answers <u>of</u>^{*wc*} the homework questions.

Correct: My math teacher always praised me when I gave the correct answers <u>to</u> the homework questions.

Incorrect: Jaime gets frustrated if he makes the same error time <u>by</u>^{*wc*} time.

Correct: Jaime gets frustrated if he makes the same error time <u>after</u> time.

Self-help Strategy: Because the rules for preposition use are very limited, you may frequently have to ask a native speaker for help. However, since some rules do exist, it is a good idea not only to learn the rules below but also to read about preposition use in an ESL grammar text. You can also improve your control of prepositions by noticing them when you read and listening for them when people speak.

Guidelines for Using Prepositions

You will find the following charts helpful for using prepositions that indicate time, place, or position:

Preposition	Time	Example
in	month, year	in February, in 1993
on	day of the week, date	on Monday, on June 1
in	time of day	in the morning, in the afternoon, in the evening (but **at** night)
at	specific time of day	at 8:00 A.M., at 3:30 sharp

Preposition	Place	Example
in	city, country	in Dallas, in Canada
on	street	on First Street
at	address	at 1119 Harvard Drive
in	inside of a place	in the language lab, in the library
at	a specific place	at school, at home, at the airport, at the store, at the movies

Preposition	Position	Example
on	on top of	on the desk, on the bed
in	inside	in my room, in my desk

PROBLEM 3. An incorrect preposition has been used following an adjective or a noun.

Note: A preposition following a verb is treated as a verb form and can be found in *Unit 2*.

Incorrect: I sometimes feel <u>uncomfortable in</u> speaking up in class.

Correct: I sometimes feel <u>uncomfortable about</u> speaking up in class.

Incorrect: My mother worked, so the <u>responsibility of</u> the housework was mine.

Correct: My mother worked, so the <u>responsibility for</u> the housework was mine.

Self-help Strategy: You can solve many of these problems by looking up the adjective or noun in an ESL dictionary.

Example: I am happy about getting a part-time job. (In this sentence, the preposition *about* is used with the adjective *happy*. An ESL dictionary would indicate that *about* can be used with *happy*.)

PROBLEM 4. A word has been used that does not exist in English.

Incorrect: The article was fairly easy to read and <u>comprehenced</u>.

Correct: The article was fairly easy to read and <u>comprehend</u>.

Incorrect: Being a student is <u>literarily</u> a full-time job.

Correct: Being a student is <u>literally</u> a full-time job.

Self-help Strategy: You can avoid many of these errors by looking up the word in a dictionary.

PROBLEM 5. **A verb has been used that does not fit the subject and/or predicate.**

> *Note*: This serious error in word choice affects the subject and/or predicate of the sentence and affects meaning, making it a global error. This error is also a common error for native speakers of English and is treated in handbooks for native speakers. Such errors may sometimes be marked **predication** or **faulty predication**.

Incorrect: Reading <u>collaborated</u> in opening Andrew's mind to a better understanding of the lives of the people around him.
(Reading cannot collaborate.)

Correct: Reading helped Andrew better understand the lives of the people around him.

Incorrect: Reiko's mother <u>suffered</u> a struggle to balance work and family.
(A struggle cannot be suffered.)

Correct: Reiko's mother suffered when struggling to balance work and family.

Self-help Strategy: To avoid predication errors, you need to make sure that the subject or predicate and the verb fit together; that is, you need to verify that the verb you have chosen can do the action required by the subject or predicate. To correct a predication error, you need to change the verb, rewrite the subject or predicate, or rewrite the whole sentence.

■ PART III: Exercises

In Part III, you will practice

- *recognizing and correcting word-choice errors in individual sentences*
- *recognizing word-choice errors in a paragraph*
- *testing your ability to choose words correctly*
- *identifying effective word use in a reading*

EXERCISE I   (Do this exercise on your own. Then check your answers with a classmate.)

Directions: Each of the following sentences has a word-choice error. Test your ability to identify incorrect words by underlining each error and then correcting it.

A. **Word-choice errors with words other than prepositions.**

1. Arturo called to say he would be late; in the meanwhile, I read a book.

2. Apartments are so expensive that his family has to cramp into a two-room apartment.

3. Her excellence in teaching has earned her spotlights.

4. I once was in a math class where everyone was motivated to conquer the best test score.

5. When Samir cannot answer in class, he feels shrink.

6. Jennifer's bad grade on her final exam in French unabled her from passing the course.

7. I became so courteous that I decided to investigate the noise.

8. Students are also putting their part in keeping the school clean by not littering.

9. During the first few months of school, I was speakless both in class and at lunchtime because of my inability to speak English.

10. After she had been studying English for six weeks, Madeleine expected to know everything, but in replacement she found she had just begun.

B. **Word-choice errors with prepositions.** If you are having difficulty deciding which prepositions should be used in these sentences, try looking up the word that comes before the preposition in a dictionary for advanced ESL learners or review the chart in *Part II* if the preposition is one of time, place, or position.

1. They had to be nice with their neighbors.

2. My brother is a student in Harvard University, and I am a student at the music department in the University of Michican.

3. The revised schedule gives students a choice with dates and times.

4. All the graduate classes in the education department are held at the early afternoon and evening.

5. It's easy to clean the kitchen when all you do is load dishes to the dishwasher.

6. My lab partner lives in 1003 Rosemont Avenue.

7. Living in an apartment is difficult if you are not happy of your roommates.

8. If you are hunting for your car keys, I saw them lying in the table.

9. If my trip goes as planned, I will see you at Monday.

10. My uncle, who owns a successful business, has had a big influence in me.

EXERCISE 2 (Do this exercise with a classmate.)

Directions: This paragraph, which was written by a student, has been edited so that the only errors are in word choice. Read the whole paragraph. Then underline each word you think has been used incorrectly. With your partner, decide on the correct word. If you are unsure, check the word in an ESL dictionary that shows usage. The first one has been done for you.

When I was a senior in high school, I dreamed about being a college student and often wondered what college would <u>appear</u>. *be like* I also wondered about how much difference there would be between college and high school, particularly in class size. I assisted to a big-city high school, which was crowded; each class had an enrollment of 40 students. Therefore, when I sent in my application for college, I hoped that classes in college would be small. However, here at college, especially for chemistry and economics classes, the class halls are overcrowded. For instance, my chemistry class has more than 300 pupils in it and some of them cannot get a seat when they come late. Some students stand at the back door, and others sit at the alley. Unfortunately, when a class is very crowded, I cannot focus on what the teacher is saying and I do not feel satisified of what I am learning. My hope that classes would be small in college has not been realized.

After you have finished the exercise, answer the following questions:

1. Which word-choice problems make this paragraph difficult to read?
2. Which word-choice errors are less disruptive?

EXERCISE 3 (Do this exercise on your own. Then check your answers with a classmate.)

Directions: Make a list of ten words commonly used either in your major or in a field that interests you. Write sentences in which you use these words. Check your answers with a classmate, preferably one who knows your field.

EXERCISE 4 (Do this exercise on your own. Then share your answers with a classmate. If you are unsure of your answers, check them with your instructor.)

Directions: Read a short article in a newspaper or a magazine and underline any words that are new to you. Then check the meaning of each new word in a dictionary, preferably an ESL dictionary with sample sentences. After determining the meaning of the word, write a sentence in which you use it.

■ PART IV: Writing Activity

In Part IV, you will
* *plan and write a response to a selected topic*
* *share your writing with a classmate*
* *edit your writing for content and sentence-level accuracy*

Step 1—Choosing a Writing Topic

Select one or both of the following:

Topic A: Think of some strategies that you would like to try to improve your English skills. Then write about the two or three you think would most help you, indicating to the reader how and why you think they will work for you.

Topic B: In a newspaper article, a recent immigrant complained that although he was taking English classes, he felt so isolated that he resorted to calling toll-free 800 numbers just to hear someone speak English and to talk to someone in English. His complaint about feeling isolated is shared by many language learners who often feel that the classroom gives them their only opportunity to use their new language. Discuss how ESL students can find opportunities to use their English, both oral and written.

Step 2—Gathering Information

With a classmate or in a small group, discuss strategies that you would like to try in order to improve your English skills. Alternatively, discuss opportunities that ESL students can find to practice their oral and written English.

Step 3—Prewriting

Working by yourself, list two or three strategies that you would like to try to help you improve your English skills OR two or three opportunities ESL students can find to practice their oral and written English. Under each strategy or opportunity, jot down examples that illustrate your point.

Step 4—Writing Your First Draft

Use your list from prewriting to help you write your first draft. Focus on content.

Step 5—Sharing Your Draft

Working with a classmate, read each other's draft. Give feedback to each other by completing the following:

A. Reading for Content
1. What did you like most about this piece of writing?
2. What would you still like to know more about?
3. What suggestions do you have for the writer?

B. Checking for Errors with Word Choice
1. Circle any errors with word choice you notice on your classmate's draft.
2. Discuss how to correct them.

Step 6—Revising Your Writing

Using your classmate's suggestions as well as your own ideas for revising, write your second draft. Focus on content and sentence-level accuracy. In particular, check the words you have chosen and correct any errors in word choice.

Step 7—Proofreading Your Final Draft

Read your final draft once again, looking in particular at your choice of words. Make any necessary changes.

Postwriting Activity

Step 1—When your response is returned, check to see if your instructor has marked any errors in word choice.

Step 2—If so, review the material in *Part II* of this unit.

Step 3—Correct each word-choice error by rewriting the sentence that contains the error. If you are unsure of the answer, ask your instructor for help.

■ PART V: Applying What You Have Learned to Other Writing Assignments

In Part V, you will

● *look for and correct errors with word choice in any other writing assignments you have done*

If you are in a composition class or another class in which you do writing, take your last returned paper and follow these directions:

1. Check whether your instructor has marked any errors in word choice on your paper. If so, try to correct them, using the material you have learned in this unit as a guide.

2. If your instructor has not marked any errors in word choice on your paper, take one paragraph and underline ten words. Try to determine whether the words convey the exact meaning that you intended. You may want to consult a dictionary. If you are not sure, ask a classmate or your instructor to help you.

3. When you do writing assignments in the future, be sure to check for errors in word choice.

UNIT 14: WORD FORM*

*wf = grading symbol for word-form errors

221

■ PART I: What You Need to Know About Errors in Word Form

In Part I, you will answer the following questions:
- *What is an error in word form?*
- *Why is it important to avoid word-form errors in writing?*
- *What are some strategies for mastering word forms?*

Definition of the Error

A word-form error (**wf**) is one in which the incorrect part of speech has been used. For example, in the sentence *I had a happiness day*, the adjective *happy* should be used instead of the noun *happiness*.

A word in English can have several different forms, depending on whether the word functions as a noun, verb, adjective, or adverb. Examine the following forms of the word *success*; notice how each form has a different grammatical function.

- His <u>success</u> surprised everyone. (noun)
- She has been <u>successful</u> in persuading others of her point of view. (adjective)
- I certainly hope she <u>succeeds</u>! (verb)
- The athlete could hardly believe that she had finished the race <u>successfully</u>. (adverb)

Errors with participles are also covered in this unit. For example, the sentence, *I am <u>interesting</u> in molecular genetics*, is incorrect because the past participle *interested* should be used rather than the present participle *interesting*. In addition, the sentence *The car is <u>rust</u>* is incorrect because the *-ed* ending has been left off the past participle. The correct form is *rusted*.

Errors in which main verbs are used instead of [*be* + past participle] are also covered in this unit. For example, the sentence, *I <u>interest</u> in the lecture*, is incorrect because the main verb *interest* does not fit here. Instead, the correct sentence is either *I <u>am interested</u> in the lecture* or *The lecture <u>interests</u> me*. Note that in the second option, the subject of the sentence must be changed from *I* to *the lecture*.

Importance of Mastering Word Forms in Writing

Academic and professional writers are expected to be able to use word forms correctly. Although word-form errors are classified as local (less serious) errors because they affect individual clauses rather than larger parts of a text, they are highly noticeable to the reader. Thus, ESL writers need to be aware that numerous word-form errors will cause a piece of writing to appear flawed to the reader.

Suggestions for Mastering Word Forms

When you are unsure whether you are using the correct form of a word, a good strategy is to look up the word in a dictionary to check what its different forms are. Most dictionaries, ESL or non-ESL, indicate the part of speech (noun, verb, adjective, adverb) next to a word. Another strategy is to become aware of common word endings that identify words as nouns, verbs, adjectives, or adverbs. For example, *-ness* is a common noun ending, *-ous* is a common adjective ending, and *-ly* is a common adverb ending. A list of some of the most common word endings is included in this unit.

You can also become aware of word formation when you read in English. For example, look carefully at several sentences in one of your textbooks, a newspaper, or a magazine. Analyze these sentences, making sure you can identify nouns, verbs, adjectives, and adverbs in each sentence. If you are having difficulty distinguishing these parts of speech, you may need to ask your instructor or a tutor for assistance.

TEST YOUR UNDERSTANDING OF WORD FORMS

After you have read *Part I*, write answers to the following questions. Share your answers with another student.

1. What is a word-form error? Explain in your own words.
2. How serious are word-form errors? Explain your answer.
3. How frequently do you make word-form errors when you write in English? Do you find yourself guessing at the form of a word rather than verifying it in a dictionary?
4. What strategies can you use to avoid word-form errors?

■ PART II: Common Problems, Rules, and Self-help Strategies

> *In Part II, you will*
> * study six problems ESL writers commonly have with word forms
> * review common noun, adjective, adverb, and verb suffixes (endings attached to words)
> * learn selected rules and self-help strategies that will help you avoid word-form errors

This section presents six problems ESL writers commonly have with word forms. First, study each problem and the examples that illustrate it. Then mark the problems you think you have when you write in English. Remember that if you become aware of the type of word-form errors you most often make, you will increase your chances of avoiding these errors in your writing.

In addition to these six problems, you will find a list of common word suffixes at the end of this section.

PROBLEM I. The choice of a word is correct, but the incorrect part of speech has been used. (*Note*: Part of speech = noun, verb, adjective, or adverb)

Incorrect: She was <u>easy</u> *wf* persuaded to change her vote.

Correct: She was <u>easily</u> persuaded to change her vote.
(An adverb instead of an adjective is needed to modify the verb *persuaded*.)

Incorrect: People tend to live a satisfying life when their <u>marriage</u> *wf* life is full of understanding and love.

Correct: People tend to live a satisfying life when their <u>married</u> life is full of understanding and love.
(An adjective instead of a noun is needed to modify the noun *life.*)

Incorrect: The students will clearly feel the <u>lost</u> *wf* of Mr. Jensen, who will no longer be teaching here.

Correct: The students will clearly feel the <u>loss</u> of Mr. Jensen, who will no longer be teaching here.
(A noun instead of an adjective is needed as the direct object of the verb *feel.*)

Incorrect: Her attitude is a <u>reflect</u> *wf* of the views of society.
Correct: Her attitude is a <u>reflection</u> of the views of society.
             (A noun instead of a verb is needed in this position.)

PROBLEM 2. A suffix has been used incorrectly.

Incorrect: I am applying to the Department of Management and
             <u>Financement</u> *wf*.
Correct: I am applying to the Department of Management and <u>Finance</u>.
Incorrect: I studied <u>hardly</u> *wf* before I took the TOEFL exam.
Correct: I studied <u>hard</u> before I took the TOEFL exam.

Self-help Strategy 1: There are no rules that will tell you whether a word requires a specific suffix to mark it as a certain part of speech. For example, the noun form of the verb *manage* in the first example sentence under Problem 2 requires the *-ment* ending, while the verb *finance* does not require an ending to form the noun *finance*. To verify word forms that you are unsure of, check your dictionary.

Self-help Strategy 2: While most adverbs have an *-ly* ending, remember that three common adverbs, *hard, last,* and *fast,* do not have this *-ly* ending.

Common Word Suffixes

This list will help you recognize common noun, verb, adjective, and adverb suffixes. Study this list. For each suffix, add at least one additional word that has the same suffix.

Noun Suffixes

-ment	argument	establishment	_____
-ness	sadness	messiness	_____
-tion	application	indication	_____
-sion	expression	admission	_____
-ity	legibility	impossibility	_____
-ence	difference	excellence	_____
-ance	importance	distance	_____
-ure	departure	closure	_____
-er	teacher	speaker	_____

Noun Suffixes, *continued*

-ism	socialism	sexism	_____
-ist	specialist	typist	_____
-ship	scholarship	friendship	_____

Verb Suffixes

-ate	mediate	delegate	_____
-en	lengthen	brighten	_____
-ify	solidify	intensify	_____
-ize	finalize	customize	_____

Adjective Suffixes

-ous	dangerous	famous	_____
-ful	colorful	useful	_____
-less	colorless	useless	_____
-ive	expressive	competitive	_____
-able	agreeable	understandable	_____
-ent	different	excellent	_____
-ant	important	hesitant	_____
-ic	characteristic	electric	_____
-al	emotional	musical	_____
-some	worrisome	bothersome	_____
-ate	considerate	subordinate	_____
-y	dressy	noisy	_____
-ly	friendly	lonely	_____
-like	childlike	ladylike	_____
-an	American	Italian	_____
-ese	Japanese	Maltese	_____
-ing	interesting	challenging	_____
-ed	interested	challenged	_____

Adverb Suffix

-ly	usually	legibly	_____

PROBLEM 3. An incorrect adjective or adverb form has been used in a comparison.

Incorrect: That was the <u>worse</u> [wf] movie I have seen in a long time.
Correct: That was the <u>worst</u> movie I have seen in a long time.

Incorrect: This semester, Faizah has been <u>more</u> [wf] busier than usual.
Correct: This semester, Faizah has been <u>busier</u> than usual.

Incorrect: Mario is working <u>hard</u> [wf] this year than last year.
Correct: Mario is working <u>harder</u> this year than last year.

Self-help Strategy: Learn the patterns that adjectives and adverbs generally follow when they are used in comparisons. Learn both the comparative and the superlative forms outlined below.

a. One-syllable adjectives and adverbs: Add [*-er + than*] for the comparative and [*the + -est*] for the superlative.

   Examples: Some students think that short-answer tests are <u>harder than</u> multiple-choice tests.
   Some students think that essay tests are <u>the hardest</u>.
   My roommate usually stays up <u>later</u> than I do.
   Monica stays up <u>the latest</u> of all my friends.

b. Most adjectives and adverbs of two or more syllables: Use [*more . . . than*] for the comparative and [*the most*] for the superlative.

   Examples: The Mexican restaurant downtown is <u>more popular than</u> the Chinese restaurant.
   The Vietnamese restaurant is <u>the most popular</u>.

c. Two-syllable words that end in *-y*: Change the *-y* to *-i*. Then add [*-er + than*] for the comparative and [*the + -est*] for the superlative.

   Examples: The red car is <u>sportier than</u> the blue car.
   The black convertible is <u>the sportiest</u> of all.

d. The following words have irregular comparative and superlative forms.

good	*better than*	*the best*
bad	*worse than*	*the worst*
little	*less than*	*the least*
much/many	*more than*	*the most*

   Examples: I like my chemistry class <u>better than</u> my math class.
   I like my history class <u>the best</u> of all.

I am earning <u>less</u> money this year <u>than</u> last year.

Of all my friends, Juan earns <u>the least</u> money.

Jogging three times a week is <u>better</u> exercise <u>than</u> swimming once a week.

The <u>best</u> exercise program is a daily workout.

PROBLEM 4. The incorrect present or past participle has been used as an adjective.

Incorrect: The essay was <u>interested</u>.

Correct: The essay was <u>interesting.</u>

Incorrect: The <u>interesting</u> students stayed after class to discuss the matter further.

Correct: The <u>interested</u> students stayed after class to discuss the matter further.

Rules for Choosing the Appropriate Participle as an Adjective

1. Use the past participle form of the verb when you are describing something or someone that is affected by someone or something else.

   Examples: The reader was <u>interested</u> in the essay.

   An <u>interested</u> reader can read for hours.

   (The focus is on the reader's being affected by the essay.)

2. Use the present participle form of the verb when you are describing something that affects someone or something else.

   Examples: The essay was <u>interesting</u>.

   An <u>interesting</u> essay holds the reader's attention.

   (The focus is on the essay's being interesting.)

PROBLEM 5. A main verb has been incorrectly used instead of [*be* + past participle].

Incorrect: I <u>concerned</u> about getting a good grade on my chemistry midterm.

Correct: I <u>am concerned</u> about getting a good grade on my chemistry midterm.

Incorrect: I <u>confuse</u> about what you just said.

Correct: I <u>am confused</u> about what you just said.

Self-help Strategy: Notice that in the preceding examples the past participle functions as an adjective. This construction is also sometimes called the stative passive. Some of these stative passive constructions can be made active by changing the word order.

a. I <u>am confused</u> about what you just said. (stative passive)

b. What you just said <u>confuses</u> me. (active voice construction)

a. I <u>am concerned</u> about getting a good grade. (stative passive)

b. Getting a good grade <u>concerns</u> me. (active voice construction)

a. San Francisco <u>is located</u> on the northern coast of California. (stative passive)

b. (No active voice construction is possible.)

PROBLEM 6. The *-ed* ending has been left off a past participle used as an adjective.

Incorrect: I was <u>impress</u> with the candidate's speech.

Correct: I was <u>impressed</u> with the candidate's speech.

Incorrect: The store is <u>close</u> on Sundays.

Correct: The store is <u>closed</u> on Sundays.

Self-help Strategy: The majority of verbs have past participles that end in *-ed*. In speaking, this *-ed* ending is sometimes hard to hear. Remember not to leave off this *-ed* ending when you write.

■ PART III: Exercises

In Part III, you will practice

- *adding appropriate suffixes to words*
- *recognizing and correcting word-form errors in sentences*
- *using present and past participles correctly as adjectives*
- *recognizing and correcting word-form errors in paragraphs*

EXERCISE 1 (Do this exercise on your own. Then check your answers with a classmate.)

Directions: Check your knowledge of word formation and suffixes by filling in the blanks with the forms of the following words commonly used by academic and professional writers.

Noun	Verb	Adjective	Adverb
theory	*theorize*	*theoretical*	*theoretically*
1. characteristic	_____	_____	_____
2. approximation	_____	_____	_____
3. prediction	_____	_____	_____
4. dependence	_____	_____	_____
5. production	_____	_____	_____
6. origin	_____	_____	_____
7. sufficiency	_____	_____	_____
8. emphasis	_____	_____	_____
9. specification	_____	_____	_____
10. significance	_____	_____	_____

EXERCISE 2 (Do this exercise on your own. Then check your answers with a classmate.)

Directions: Examine the following sentences. First, decide if a sentence is correct (C) or if it contains any word-form errors (I). Then correct the incorrect word forms.

Example: __I__ The young child did not receive much <u>encourage</u> to speak her native language. *(encouragement)*

_____ 1. Writing under the pressure of time gives us several beneficial including the ability to think fast and to organize fast.

_____ 2. I appreciate it when my parents do not interfere with my life.

_____ 3. Many immigrants become maturity by dealing with adult problems at an early age.

_____ 4. China is located in center Asia.

_____ 5. I don't see why a young child should be punished harsh.

_____ 6. Ora came to the United States to pursuit her Ph.D.

_____ 7. In order to success, one must be able to make sacrifices.

_____ 8. Antonio is an immigrant from Portugal.

_____ 9. My suggest is aimed at easing the problem.

_____ 10. If I keep writing in this fashion, my writing skills might even become worst, for I might get used to making those mistakes.

_____ 11. When my husband cooks, I have to clean up the messiness he makes.

_____ 12. His answer was an emphatic no.

EXERCISE 3 (Do this exercise on your own. Then check your answers with a classmate.)

Directions: Check your ability to use present and past participles as adjectives by filling in the blanks with the correct form of the verb indicated.

Examples: Writing in English is quite __challenging__ (challenge) to me.
I am __confused__ (confuse) about what the lecturer meant by some of his statements.

---

1. I am _____ (excite) about the party.

2. My professor's absence was _____ (surprise) to all of us in the class.

3. The room, with its chipping paint, leaking roof, and lack of light, was _____ (depress).

4. Mario is _____ (interest) in the topic of the lecture because it is related to his research.

5. Natalie was _____ (puzzle) by the grade she received on her midterm.

6. Your ability to type quickly and accurately is _____ (amaze).

7. I was _____ (depress) when I saw my grade.

8. The amount of money raised by the walkathon was _____ (astonish).

9. Jack was completely _____ (surprise) by the party his friends gave for him.

10. This book is one of the most _____ (entertain) books that I have ever read.

EXERCISE 4 (Do this exercise with a classmate.)

Directions: The following paragraph, written by a student about the benefits of being bilingual, contains errors in word form. Underline each word-form error and write the correct form of the word above it.

My bilingualism may benefit me in terms of job opportunities. First of all, more and more <u>immigrates</u> *immigrants* arrive in the United States every year. To help these new immigrates or to do business with them, bilingual and multilingual employees are needed. For example, banks, law firms, and insurance agencies often need employees who can communicative with both non-English speakers and English-speaking clients. Therefore, because I speak Spanish good, I might find many job opportunities in places where there are a lot of Spanish speakers, such as Los Angeles, New York, Chicago, and Miami. Secondly, if I can achievement my goal of having my own dentist clinic, Spanish-speaking clients may be a good source for my earns. Many Spanish speakers tendency to feel more comfort with Spanish-speaking doctors and dentists. Even Mexicans and Mexican-Americans who speak English very well often still preference to go to Spanish-speaking dentists instead of English-speaking dentists. So, overall, I may benefit economical from my knowledgement of two languages.

EXERCISE 5 (Do this exercise on your own. Then check your answers with a classmate.)

Directions: The following paragraph, written by a student, contains errors in word form. Underline each word-form error and write the correct form of the word above it.

Being multilingual enables me to communicate <u>direct</u> *directly* with many people. Even though I mostly use English in my everyday life, especially at the university, I still use Cantonese to communicate with my relatives. My grandmother, for example, who just recently came to the United States from Vietnam and is now living with my family, cannot understand English. The only language she speaks fluent is Cantonese. Therefore, knowing how to speak Cantonese allows me to communicate easy with her. By talking with her, I have learned some of my family's historical. She told me that she and my grandfather were originally from China and she explanation what her life was like there. She has also told me interest stories about China that I never would have heard if I could not speak Cantonese. Moreover, being able to speak Cantonese or Vietnamese in Chinese and Vietnamese restaurants has also been benefit to me. The restaurant employees recognize that they and I are from similar backgrounds because we speak the same language. They, therefore, give more attentive to me than to customers who do not speak the language. Thus, being able to speak these languages opens the door for me to communication closely with many different people.

EXERCISE 6 (Do this exercise on your own. Then check your answers with a classmate.)

Directions: Read a short article from a newspaper or a magazine. Then underline all of the words with noun, verb, adjective, or adverb suffixes in two paragraphs of the article. Identify the part of speech (noun, verb, adjective, or adverb) of each word you have underlined.

■ PART IV: Writing Activity

> ### *In Part IV, you will*
> - *plan and write a response to a selected topic*
> - *share your writing with a classmate*
> - *edit your writing for content and sentence-level accuracy*

Step 1—Choosing a Writing Topic

Select one or more of the following:

Topic A: Write about a person whom you admire. This person can be a well-known contemporary figure, a historical figure, or someone you know. Explain why you admire this person.

Topic B: Write about the most challenging or interesting class you are taking. First, describe the class, including what is covered in the class and what is expected of you as a student. Then explain why it is challenging or interesting to you.

Step 2—Gathering Information

Discuss your topic with a classmate or in a small group. If you have chosen Topic A, discuss the people you each admire. Talk about the qualities of these people and the reasons you admire them. If you have selected Topic B, discuss the most challenging or interesting class you are taking. Discuss the scope of the class and the requirements for students.

Step 3—Prewriting

Working by yourself, list some of the ideas you have discussed. For Topic A, make some notes on the person you have chosen. Who is this person? What are some of his or her personal qualities? Why do you admire that person? For Topic B, make some notes about the class you will write about. List reasons it is either interesting or challenging.

Step 4—Writing Your First Draft

Use your notes from prewriting to help you write your first draft. Focus on content.

Step 5—Sharing Your Draft

Working with a classmate, read each other's draft. Give feedback to each other by answering these questions:

A. Reading for Content
  1. What do you like most about this paper?
  2. What would you still like to know more about?
  3. What suggestions do you have for the writer?
B. Reading for Word-Form Errors
  1. Circle any word-form errors in your classmate's draft.
  2. Discuss how to correct them.

Step 6—Revising Your Writing

Using your classmate's suggestions as well as your own ideas for revising, write your second draft. Focus on content and sentence-level accuracy.

Step 7—Proofreading Your Final Draft

Read your final draft once again, paying particular attention to word forms. Make any necessary changes.

Postwriting Activity

Step 1—When your response is returned, check to see if your instructor has marked any errors in word form.

Step 2—If so, review the material in *Part II* of this unit.

Step 3—Correct each word-form error by rewriting the sentence.

■ PART V: Applying What You Have Learned to Other Writing Assignments

In Part V, you will

- *look for and correct word-form errors in other writing assignments*

If you are in a composition class or another class in which you do writing assignments, take your last returned paper and follow these directions:

1. Check whether your instructor has marked any word-form errors on your paper. If so, try to correct them, using what you have learned in this unit.
2. If your instructor has not marked any word-form errors, take a paragraph and underline several words. Determine whether these words are correctly formed.
3. When you are writing in the future, be sure to check for word-form errors.

UNIT 15: NONIDIOMATIC*

*nonidiom = grading symbol for nonidiomatic writing

■ PART I: What You Need to Know About Nonidiomatic Writing

> **In Part I, you will answer the following questions:**
> - *What is nonidiomatic writing?*
> - *Why is it important to avoid nonidiomatic writing?*
> - *What are some strategies for mastering idiomatic English?*

Definition of the Error

In nonidiomatic writing (**nonidiom**), the message of a phrase or sentence is clear but a native speaker would not phrase the idea that way. For example, in the sentence *When I write under pressure, I feel that <u>I lack of knowledge of expressing myself with sophisticated English words</u>*, the underlined part is not written in idiomatic English. A native speaker might phrase the sentence in this way: *When I write under pressure I feel that <u>I cannot use sophisticated English words to express myself</u>* or *<u>I lack the knowledge to express myself in sophisticated English</u>*.

   Nonidiomatic differs from *unclear* in that the reader can usually grasp the meaning in a nonidiomatic phrase or sentence but not in an unclear phrase or sentence. Although *nonidiomatic* is usually a local (less serious) error, if too much of a piece of writing is nonidiomatic, the error can become global (more serious).

   Errors with idiomatic expressions differ from nonidiomatic writing. Idiomatic expressions are set words or phrases that are commonly used and that can be found in a dictionary of idioms or a text that focuses on idioms. Various errors can occur with idiomatic expressions. For example, in the sentence *I would rather use a computer than write by a hand, by a hand* should be *by hand*, an article error. In the sentence *I make the same mistakes in English times after times, times after times* should be *time after time*, a number error.

Importance of Mastering Idiomatic English in Writing

When reading nonidiomatic phrases or sentences, the reaction of the native speaker often is: "I can understand what the writer is saying, but it sounds 'funny' to me." Not only do ESL writers need to master idiomatic English so that their writing does not sound foreign to a native speaker, but they also need to keep in mind that the closer their writing is to idiomatic English, the easier it is for the reader to understand.

Suggestions for Mastering Idiomatic English

Improving your mastery of idiomatic English is a difficult task because idiomatic English is not based on rules but rather on usage. Therefore, the degree to which you master idiomatic English depends, to a great extent, on your commitment to using English and your desire to write like a native speaker.

Although mastering idiomatic English may seem like an enormous task, you can make this mastery much easier by attempting it in small chunks. For example, you could first focus on using more idiomatic English in your major or your field of interest, the field in which you are most likely to be doing the majority of your writing.

Five concrete suggestions for improving your command of idiomatic writing are as follows:

1. Read in English as much as possible.
2. Listen attentively to the way English is used.
3. Think in English as much as possible rather than translate.
4. Realize native speakers use their language in ways that cannot be taught but that you, as a nonnative speaker, must acquire to improve your command of English.
5. When a phrase or sentence in your paper has been marked nonidiomatic and you are unsure how to reword it, ask a native speaker how he or she would say it. Then rewrite that sentence or phrase, and memorize it for later use.

TEST YOUR UNDERSTANDING
OF NONIDIOMATIC WRITING

After you have read *Part I*, write answers to the following questions. Share your answers with another student.

1. What is nonidiomatic writing? Explain in your own words.
2. Why can nonidiomatic writing be a local error (less serious) or a global error (more serious)?
3. Do you think in English when you write? Why should ESL writers try to think in English as much as possible when they write? Explain your answer.
4. What suggestions do you think will best help you improve your command of idiomatic English?

■ PART II: Examples of Nonidiomatic Writing

The following nonidiomatic sentences were taken from students' writing. The correct version of each sentence is only a suggestion; in nonidiomatic sentences, often several versions may be correct depending on what the writer wanted to say. Unlike *unclear*, however, the general meaning of the sentence is always understandable.

Incorrect: Because the next history test is worth 100 points, I will have to
              nonidiom
              study <u>to my fullest</u>.

Correct: Because the history test is worth 100 points, I will have to study <u>very hard</u>.

              nonidiom
Incorrect: <u>The residential students</u> waved and smiled at me.

Correct: <u>The students in the residence halls</u> waved and smiled at me.

Incorrect: I like to study on the first floor of the library because of the <u>vast</u>
              nonidiom
              <u>bloodline</u> of people I can see entering the library.

Correct: I like to study on the first floor of the library because of the <u>variety</u> of people I can see entering the library.

                                                          nonidiom
Incorrect: Writing compositions for my French class is <u>causing me</u>
              <u>struggles</u>.

Correct: Writing compositions for my French class is <u>difficult for me</u>.

Correct: Writing compositions for my French class is <u>a struggle for me</u>.

■ PART III: Exercise

To see how well you can recognize nonidiomatic English, do the exercise below. Only one exercise is given in this unit because patterns of nonidiomatic errors differ from writer to writer, depending on many factors, including to what degree the writer is translating directly from his or her native language to English.

EXERCISE (Do this exercise on your own. Then check your answers with a classmate.)

Directions: Test your ability to recognize nonidiomatic English by underlining the nonidiomatic parts of these sentences and then rewriting them in idiomatic English.

> **Example:** *Based on my experience*
> ~~As my feeling~~ during the last year, the biggest challenge for a new university student is gaining confidence to participate fully in class discussions.

1. My mother did not let us go to the mall alone when we were small ages.

2. By talking to native speakers, I can have a little bit of knowledge about American customs.

3. According to an essay in *Time* for May 20th issue, job openings for college graduates dropped ten percent in the 1990–91 academic year.

4. That red blouse doesn't suit of those purple jeans.

5. My aunt, who lives in Los Angeles, takes the bus everywhere because she is afraid to drive freeway.

6. Now that my English has improved, I can make communication with my friends.

7. After talking with my teacher, I am more understanding of the lecture.

8. It was blowing very hard and then the wind died down in a sudden.

Index